Risk Management

Health and Safety in Primary Care

GW00503151

*This book is dedicated to the memory of
the sixteen children who died innocently in March 1996
at Dunblane Primary School.*

Risk Management

Health and Safety in Primary Care

Nigel Higson
MA BM BCh DRCOG
General Medical Practitioner

Butterworth-Heinemann
Linacre House, Jordan Hill, Oxford OX2 8DP
A division of Reed Educational and Professional Publishing Ltd

 A member of the Reed Elsevier plc group

OXFORD   BOSTON   JOHANNESBURG
MELBOURNE   NEW DELHI   SINGAPORE

First published 1996
© Reed Educational and Professional Publishing Ltd 1996

British Library Cataloguing in Publication Data

A catalogue record for this book is available from The British Library.

Library of Congress Cataloguing in Publication Data

A catalogue record for this book is available from The Library of Congress.

ISBN 0 7506 3064 7

Composition by Scribe Design, Gillingham, Kent
Printed and bound in Great Britain by Biddles Ltd, Guildford and King's Lynn

Contents

At Butterworth-Heinemann we are determined to provide you with a quality service. To help supply you with information on relevant titles as soon as it is available, please fill in the form below and return to us using the FREEPOST facility. Thank you for your help and we look forward to hearing from you.

What title have you purchased? _____

Where was the purchase made ? _____

When was the purchase made? _____

Name (Please Print): _____

Job Title: _____

Street: _____

Town: _____

County: _____ Postcode: _____

Country: _____ Telephone: _____

Company Activity: _____

Signature: _____ Date: _____

* Please arrange for me to be kept informed of other books, journals and information services on this and related subjects (* delete if not required). This in ormation is being collected on behalf of Reed International Books Ltd and may be used to supply information about products produced by companies within the Reed International Books group.

(FOR OFFICE USE ONLY)

Butterworth-Heinemann Limited – Registered Office: Michelin House, 81 Fulham Road, London, SW3 6RB. Registered in England 194771. VAT number GB: 340 242992

Direct Mail Department
Butterworth-Heinemann
FREEPOST
OXFORD
OX2 8BR

UK

Introduction

The concept of risk in primary care is one which has been misunderstood by practitioners for many years. Risk has only been believed to be in relation to clinical malpractice – or 'mistakes'. The inherent risks involved in running a practice have not been considered until recently.

Many thousands upon thousands of consultations take place each and every week in the primary care setting – one that includes general practice, dentistry, chiropody, chiropractic, osteopathy, physiotherapy, not to mention the many other branches of primary care contact which include such subjects as diverse as acupuncture and reflexology. Patients entrust themselves to the care of these practitioners on the assumption that they are going to be cured, or in the least, made no worse, by such a consultation. However is this the case?

Among GPs there is still a denial of the need to have protection against hepatitis. Recent surveys have shown less than 80 per cent uptake of this highly effective vaccine among practising GPs. Although the practitioner may accept the risk of developing the disease, it is important that he considers the possibility that he might pass the disease onto patients while undertaking minor surgery or other invasive procedures. Many practices do not have effective sterilisation policies for the various instruments that they use in the working day. Staff handle clinical specimens without adequate health protection or handling training. Patients may have to sit in waiting rooms next to others infested with lice or coughing purulent sputum. Steps down to the consulting room may be greasy with leaves in the autumn, resulting in patients or staff slipping and injuring themselves.

All these risks can be assessed and managed – not necessarily prevented – thus reducing the chance of the practitioner becoming liable for increased litigation. Risks can be avoided. Those which cannot be avoided can be managed. Effective management of risk results in decreased cost of risk.

This book is written by a practising primary care practitioner. It encompasses all the necessary law and recommendations concerning health and safety at work current at the time of publication. It includes discussion of controlling substances hazardous to health (COSHH) and looks at appropriate training of staff employed in primary care. Where appropriate, each section includes a detailed policy on the appropriate management of the risks discussed – this can be adapted by the reader to use in his own practice.

References are made within the text to the Health and Safety Policy and other documents as being 'controlled documents'. This stems from the principles of document control which those familiar with quality system management will already understand. Essentially there are a certain number and type of document which are essential to the running of the business; such may include the account books, the list of suppliers, the rules and regulations imposed on the business by other authorities. The health and safety documentation falls within this group of documents and should be maintained as such with regular updating and checking that it is still appropriate to the needs and nature of the business.

Comments and suggestions are always welcome by the author and the publisher in respect of the contents and style of this book. The various professional organisations and regulatory authorities are always pleased to help with reducing the effect of risk in primary care.

My thanks to the publishers for their considerable help and advice on presentation.

1

Health and safety law

The statement of law

This is a statement which must be advised to all members of staff and displayed on the business premises. It should apply, in good practice, to all businesses and is the basis for the employee's protection. Many areas of health and safety recommendations are not obviously applicable to primary care, but they do apply to contractors working on your premises as well as regular employees. Although under a building contract you may delegate the responsibility to the contractor, you should ensure that someone has the legal liability if a brick falls onto a patient's hand during renovation work. Trailing cables and temporary structures are always temptations for children to investigate.

The statement should read:

HEALTH AND SAFETY LAW
Your employer has a duty under the law to ensure, so far as is reasonably practicable, your health, safety and welfare at work.

In general, your employer's duties include:

- Making your workplace safe and without risks to health.
- Keeping dust, fumes and noise under control.
- Ensuring plant and machinery are safe and that safe systems of work are set and followed.
- Ensuring articles and substances are moved, stored and used safely.
- Providing adequate welfare facilities.
- Giving you the information, instruction, training and supervision necessary for your health and safety.

Your employer must also:

- Draw up a health and safety policy statement if there are five or more employees, including the health and safety organisation and arrangements in force and bring it to your attention.

- Provide free, any protective clothing or equipment specifically required by health and safety law.
- Report certain injuries, disease and dangerous occurrences to the enforcing authority.
- Provide adequate first aid facilities.
- Consult a safety representative, if one is appointed by a recognised trade union, about matters affecting your health and safety.
- Set up a safety committee if asked in writing by two or more safety representatives.

Employers also have duties to take precautions against fire, provide adequate means of escape and means of fighting fires.

In many workplaces employers may have other specific duties:

- To take adequate precautions against explosions of flammable dust or gas.
- To maintain a workroom temperature of at least 16°C after the first hour of work where employees do most of their work sitting down.
- To keep the workplace clean.
- To provide, maintain and keep clean, washing and toilet facilities and accommodation for clothing and to provide drinking water.
- To ensure that floors, steps, stairs, ladders, passages and gangways are well-constructed and maintained, and not obstructed.
- To take special precautions before allowing employees to enter and work in a confined space.
- To ensure that employees do not have to lift, carry or move any load so heavy that it is likely to injure them.
- To guard securely all dangerous parts of machines.
- To see that employees, especially young people, are properly trained or under adequate supervision before using dangerous machines.
- To ensure that lifting equipment (hoists, lifts, chains, ropes, cranes and lifting tackle) and steam boilers, steam receivers and air receivers are well-constructed, well-maintained and examined at specific intervals.
- To give employees suitable eye protection or protective clothing for certain jobs.
- To take proper precautions to prevent employees being exposed to substances which may damage their health.

- To take precautions against danger from electrical equipment and radiation.

As an employee, you have legal duties too. They include:

- Taking reasonable care for your own health and safety and that of others who may be affected by what you do or do not do.
- Cooperating with your employer on health and safety.
- Not interfering with or misusing anything provided for your health safety or welfare.

If you think there is a health and safety problem in your workplace you should first discuss it with your employer, supervisor or manager. You may also wish to discuss it with your safety representative if there is one.

If the problem remains or you need more help, health and safety inspectors can give advice on how to comply with the law. They also have powers to enforce it. The Health and Safety Executive's (HSE's) Employment Medical Advisory Service can give advice on health at work and first aid. The Advisor can be contacted at:

Telephone: _____ (See under Health and Safety Executive in the Telephone Book).

You can get advice on general fire precautions from the Fire Brigade or your fire officer.

The main Act of Parliament is the Health and Safety at Work Act 1974, but for particular purposes the Factories Act 1961, the Offices, Shops and Railway Premises Act 1963, the Fire Precautions Act 1971 and other Acts and regulations made under any of these may be equally relevant.

> Text excerpt from *HSE Health and Safety Law,*
> ISBN 0 11 701425 7. Crown Copyright 1989.
> Display copies of this text may be obtained from HMSO.

It can be seen that this general statement of law concentrates on the practical, the effective and the 'common-sense'. It states that a health and safety *policy* is necessary if there are five or more employees. It can also be seen that it is the responsibility of the employer to make the necessary arrangements to prevent and to deal with injury at work.

Not only should the employer have this statement of health and safety issued to each employee and displayed on the premises, he should also have a policy regarding health and safety management for his business. Although this is only required under law if five or more staff are employed (no distinction between part time and full time), it is obviously good practice to have such a policy in any business.

The wording of policies can vary, but it is wise to include certain basic categories:

- A general statement of recognition of the employer's responsibilities
- The safety liaison officer
- Communication
- Inspections
- Accident reports and investigation
- Training
- Purchase of goods and services
- Use of contractors and their responsibilities
- Planning of developments
- Fire precautions
- Maintenance of plant and equipment
- First aid
- Protective clothing
- Waste disposal
- Job descriptions/contracts

Although I give here a general policy, the expectation is that this should serve as a discussion document for each reader to develop his or her own policy and protocols in order that it can be seen that the whole process and the concepts behind the policy areas have been considered and developed in such a way that they are appropriate to the practice's own administrative systems.

General statement of policy

The Partners (or Associates) of ____*(Insert name of practice)*____ recognise and accept their responsibility as employers for providing a safe and healthy workplace and working environment for each of their employees.

The Partners (or Associates) will use their best resources to meet this responsibility and to allocate the resources needed for the purpose, paying particular attention to safety and health in relation to:

- Place of work and access to it

- Plant, equipment and systems of work
- Arrangements for the use, handling, storage and transport of articles and substances
- The working environment
- Welfare facilities
- The provision of information, instruction, training and supervision to help all employees to avoid hazards and to contribute positively to their own safety and health at work

All aspects of this document and policy refer to the safety of members of the public and other users of the Health Care Centre.

The Partners (or Associates) recognise that no safety policy is likely to be successful unless it actively involves employees themselves. The Partners (or Associates) will therefore cooperate fully with staff safety representatives and will provide them, so far as resources allow, with facilities and training to carry out this task.

Employees are reminded of their own duties (under Section 7 of the Health and Safety at Work Act) to take care for their own safety and that of other employees and to cooperate with the Partners, Associates or Managers of the Practice so as to enable them to carry-out their own responsibilities successfully:

- By working safely and efficiently.
- By using the protective equipment provided for their own and other people's safety and by meeting statutory obligations.
- By reporting incidents that have led or may lead to injury or damage.
- By adhering to procedures laid down by management for securing a safe workplace.
- By helping in the investigation of incidents so that measures may be devised to prevent a recurrence.

A copy of this statement shall be issued to all employees. It may be revised or modified from to time and will be reviewed at least annually. The next revision being due by
_____.

Safety Liaison Officer

The Safety Liaison Officer, as required by HC(78)30 is –
_____

The functions of the Safety Liaison Officer include:

- Reviewing and coordinating implementation of the safety policy and reporting to the Partners (or Associates) of the primary care centre with recommendations for changes when necessary.
- Acting as a source of information about the formal implications of the Act.
- Maintaining contact with local Health and Safety Inspectors.
- Ensuring the distribution of guidance documents from the Health and Safety Commission and the Department of Health to relevant managers, specialist safety officers and safety representatives[1].
- Coordinating the collection of accident or incident statistics and their appropriate dissemination.
- Arranging for any necessary staff training.
- Attending any appropriate safety committees.

Communication

The Partners (or Associates) welcome ideas which may lead to the prevention of accidents or incidents and these should be discussed with the Safety Liaison Officer.

Hazard Notices

These notices are issued as and when necessary by the Department of Health to warn health care providers of possible hazards in the use of particular items of equipment. The Safety Liaison Officer will assess each notice and action appropriately. A file copy will be kept of all health hazard notices and these will be indexed within the file. The file is a controlled document and stored as such.

Inspection

The Partners (or Associates) acknowledge the present content of the Regulations concerning inspection of the workplace in that members of the management team and the Safety Liaison Officer will be entitled to make an inspection of workplaces in the following circumstances, in particular:

- Regular inspections of the workplace at three-monthly intervals, or more often where circumstances warrant it.
- Where a notifiable disease has been contracted.

- Where a part of the workplace has housed a dangerous occurrence.
- The relevant part of the workplace where there has been a substantial change in the conditions of work.
- Where new information relevant to hazards in the workplace has been published by the Health and Safety Committee or the Health and Safety Executive.
- Where there has been a complaint by an employee or other user of the premises.

Following an inspection, a report shall be prepared and signed by the Safety Liaison Officer stating the date, the parts of the workplace inspected and anything disclosed which, in the opinion of the inspectors, will be detrimental to the health and safety of persons employed in that place. The report may also make recommendations. Copies of all reports will be maintained in the controlled file designated for that purpose.

Accident reports and investigation

Where an accident or incident, however trivial, arises owing to faulty machinery, equipment, substance or situation, etc., the immediate senior partner (or Associate) present shall be informed and he or she will arrange for the fault to be remedied.

Proper records of accidents occurring to anyone on premises owned or leased by the Partners (or Associates) will be kept as a controlled document.

The Safety Liaison Officer will be notified as soon as possible of any incidents reported and he will receive a copy of written statement from any staff member or partner or other user concerned.

The Safety Liaison Officer, or in his absence, the Senior Partner (or Associate) present, will notify the Health and Safety Inspectorate where an employee sustains an accident resulting in absence from work for more than three days. It is noted that this responsibility has been extended, as a result of the Notification of Accidents and Dangerous Occurrences Regulations 1980, to include accidents involving:

- Death
- Personal Injury as defined in the regulations
- Injury resulting in an employee being incapacitated from work for more than three consecutive days excluding the day of the accident and any Sunday
- Dangerous occurrences

Training

The Partners (or Associates) recognise their legal responsibilities in training all staff on health and safety matters.

The types of training necessary are different for each post and the Safety Liaison Officer will assess the needs for each individual employee. This will be recorded on the appropriate training record sheet for each employee and all training documented.

Purchase of goods and services

The Partners (or Associates) recognise their responsibilities under Section 6 of the Health and Safety at Work Act (HSAWA) in respect of commodities supplied to the primary care centre.

The purchaser of all goods supplied for surgery use will ensure that the supplier of those goods approves,

- That the articles or substances are safe without risk to health; and
- That adequate information is supplied about conditions or use which are necessary to ensure that the articles and substances will be safe and without risk to health when properly used.

The Safety Liaison Officer will make arrangements for bringing to the attention of any person who erects or installs on the premises any article for use at work, that person's duty to ensure that nothing about the way in which an article is erected or installed makes it unsafe or a risk to health when properly used.

The Safety Liaison Officer will ensure that any information supplied about hazards which may be encountered and precautions which must be taken in connection with any articles or substances purchased by or on behalf of the Partners (or Associates) to be passed on to the persons who will use the articles or substances.

Use of contractors and their responsibilities

The Partners' (or Associates') responsibilities for the safety of people within their premises is extended by law to any contractors undertaking repairs, maintenance, installations, building, etc. within the workplace. In addition, every contractor must accept full responsibility for complying with the relevant provision of the HASAWA (Health and Safety at Work Act) and all relevant regulations in respect of work required by the contract. The Contractors shall conform with the practice's safety practices. During the currency of contract an employee or Partner (or Associate) may draw to the Contractor's attention, any working method that might create risk of injury to any person on site. The Contractor shall undertake to remedy this without delay. Contractors will be made aware of all relevant systems and will be obliged to comply with these.

Planning of developments

Planning of work, minor or major, by the Partners (or Associates) will allow at the time of pre-planning and in the tendering for work, for provision of safe systems of work and proper health and welfare arrangements during the time the work is carried out and for such proper arrangements in the completed works.

Fire precautions

A separate Fire Precautions Policy exists. (See page 48.)

Maintenance of plant and equipment

All equipment should be inspected for safety prior to purchase. The Safety Liaison Officer is responsible for the adequate maintenance of all plant and equipment after purchase. All technical specification and service records will be kept in the appropriate controlled file.

First aid

A first aid box, equipped as required by the Factories Act[2], will be kept on the surgery premises and it will be inspected monthly by a member of the management staff.

It is the policy of the Partners (or Associates) that all members of Reception Staff shall be trained in first aid as resources allow.

Protective clothing

Suitable protective clothing will be available for all members of staff requiring it.

Waste disposal

The Partners (or Associates) will conform with the regulations for controlled disposal of all waste. Duty of Care transfer notes will be maintained in the controlled file.

Job descriptions/contracts

Responsibility for health and safety will be written into all contracts.

Reading the general policy above it is obvious that there are a lot of areas which need consideration and development within any form of primary care service – control of waste, control of infection, prevention of injury, first aid boxes – to name only a few. Health and safety at work is a major problem for any employer, but effective management of potential risk can reduce that risk. Health and Safety issues should be addressed as a priority area for your business. To initiate and regulate changes, effective and practical procedural systems should be developed covering all areas of your work.

The rest of this book is designed to assist you, as a practising primary care clinician, to ensure that your work is safe both to you and your colleagues, your staff, your subcontractors and your patients. Now read on!

Notes

1   These may all be the same person in a small organisation
2   See appropriate section on First Aid

Sterilisation techniques

Surgical skill and ability apart it is essential that the patient is not exposed to any increased risk from cross infection. Similarly, the practitioner and other members of the primary care team must be protected from infection at all times. Simple procedures for instrument handling and cleaning can protect both patient and practitioner from cross contamination.

Instruments

Clean and dirty instruments must be kept totally separate in labelled containers which should be kept well above child height.

Dirty instruments must be processed by first cleaning and rinsing using household detergent and water (preferably running water). If not cleaned and rinsed in this manner, then body fluids on the instrument may coagulate and become firmly fixed to the instrument allowing a contamination site. The operator should wear household gloves and full apron/eye protection when washing instruments in this manner.

Decontamination of the instruments should follow initial cleaning. The usual methods of decontamination are:

- Steam under pressure in an autoclave
- Dry heat in a hot air oven
- Boiling water
- Chemical disinfectants

Steam under pressure

This is the most efficient way of sterilising and decontaminating instruments. As temperatures may reach 134°C this method is obviously not appropriate for plastic instruments. Autoclaves must be properly loaded and not overloaded in order for all surfaces of the instrument to be exposed to the steam. Instruments will need to cool before use but must not be used after three hours as sterility cannot be maintained even when covered with sterile paper/cloth.

The Department of Health has published an evaluation of 11 different autoclaves (Health equipment information (HEI) No. 185 July 1988). The British Standards Committee have suggested the following guidelines:

The autoclave should have a preset automatic cycle. The operation of the cycle should be fully automatic according to the temperature and time specifications:

Temperature
121°C   15 minutes
126°C   10 minutes
134°C   3 minutes

Autoclaves should offer sterilising cycles within the temperatures and times above.

The steriliser should provide indications of both the temperature and pressure within the chamber. Separate systems are required so that each provides a backup to the other.

In order to control and monitor the temperature of the steriliser when it is being serviced, the autoclave should have a thermocouple entry point.

Dry heat in a hot air oven

Hot air ovens need higher operating temperatures than do autoclaves as the sterilising ability of dry air is less than steam. Longer times are also necessary:

Temperature
160°C   60 minutes
170°C   40 minutes
180°C   20 minutes

Unless hot air ovens are fan assisted they tend to create hot and cold spots which will result in some instruments not reaching the required temperature whilst others will become too hot and damaged. A long cooling down period is required for instruments from a hot air oven.

Boiling water

Boiling water is efficient in bringing all parts of an instrument to the required temperature but will not sterilise instruments as many bacterial spores can survive at 100°C. Instruments must be fully immersed in boiling water for a minimum of five minutes after the water has returned to the boil. The water in such disinfection units should be changed daily.

Chemical disinfection

Chemical disinfection is not adequate for most instruments. Certain instruments such as gastroscopes or fibre-optic sigmoidoscopes can be effectively disinfected by the chemicals and the disinfection routines advised by the chemical manufacturer should be followed exactly.

Instrument decontamination and usage in primary care

High risk (Sterilise or 'single-use disposable instruments'.):

- Surgical scissors and forceps
- Stitch cutters
- Intrauterine device sets
- Uterine sounds
- Tenaculums
- Neurological examination pins
- Fitting Rings or diaphragms
- Dental handpieces which come into direct contact with body fluids
- Acupuncture needles

Medium risk (Sterilise or single use. Boiling if suitable is an acceptable alternative.):

- Vaginal speculums
- Fitting rings/diaphragms
- Ring pessaries
- Proctoscopes/sigmoidoscopes
- Laryngeal mirrors
- Nasal speculums
- Tongue depressors
- Peakflow meter mouthpieces

Thermometers: oral/rectal/surface: Should be soaked fully immersed in 70 per cent alcohol for 10 minutes, preferably turned at least once to ensure coating of alcohol.

Ear syringe or otoscope nozzles: Should be sterilised or boiled preferably. If not, chemical disinfection or wash.

Sigmoidoscopes: Rigid sigmoidoscopes can be easily sterilised in an autoclave after thorough cleaning. Flexible sigmoidoscopes, however, must be first cleaned and then disinfected in a glutaraldehyde solution as recommended by the British Society of Gastroenterology.

Glutaraldehyde is a noxious chemical controlled by COSHH regulations (see page 78) and should not be present in the environment in quantities above 0.2 parts per million. It is therefore preferable that appropriate equipment is available to remove the fumes or to enclose the disinfection process (either a closed automatic washer or a fume cupboard). The cost of specialist cleaning equipment is high and it is essential that practitioners who aim to provide a flexible sigmoidoscopy service to their patients should take account of the necessary health and safety aspects.

Cleaning hands

Handwashing should take place before any contact with the patient or instruments. Ordinary soap and water is adequate for low and medium risk procedures, drying with a disposable paper towel or clean hand towel.

For high risk procedures, the hands should be washed with a surgical scrub solution. Using nail brushes is not essential unless dirt is ingrained. Hands should then be dried using paper hand towels. Cuts and grazes should be covered with a waterproof adhesive dressing.

Cleaning surfaces

Wherever possible sterilisable trays should be used for instruments – failing that, a disposable cover. Work surfaces should be cleaned with a suitable alcohol or hypochlorite solution at the end of each session. If there is visible pus, blood or other body fluid, then this should be removed with a hypochlorite solution containing 10 000 parts per million available chlorine and then cleaned with a single use cloth which is then disposed to the clinical waste bag. The solution should be left on the surface for a minimum of three minutes before rinsing and drying.

Notes

Weller, I.V.D. (1988) Cleaning and disinfection of equipment for gastrointestinal flexible endoscopy: interim recommendations of a working party of the British Society of Gastroenterology. *Gut*, **29**, 1134–51.

3

Control of infection

All patients are potential carriers of hepatitis and HIV or any as yet unidentified infectious disease. Decontamination and prevention of infection must apply to each and every patient and every procedure. Latex procedure gloves are adequate against transmission of infectious diseases but are not resistant to needle or scalpel penetration. Contamination of the buccal/nasal mucosa and conjunctivae is possible during many procedures and it is advisable to wear protective clothes, masks and eye protection when undertaking any operative procedure which will include dental hygiene work.

Hepatitis

Hepatitis B immunisation is now cheaply and safely available. All medical, dental and nursing practitioners who come into contact with body fluids of patients should ensure that they receive full protection from the vaccine. Current BMA and BDA guidelines indicate that a course of hepatitis B vaccine should be given to any health worker who is at risk of infection. Antibody levels should be checked after completion of the course and if inadequate levels of antibodies are present, then a further dose of vaccine should be given. The level of antibodies should be monitored biennially and booster doses given as appropriate.

Sharps should be disposed into a suitable, specially designed receptacle. These should not be overfilled, and MUST be kept out of the reach of children. The FHSA/Medical Board reimburse the costs of sharps collection services and containers for NHS GPs. There is therefore no justifiable excuse for failure to dispose of such items sensibly.

Needle clipping devices are not safe. Such devices often leave behind a sharp hazard which is capable of passing infection. Community workers should use a British Standard Sharps container.

Clinical waste must be incinerated in a closed furnace. Various health authorities, local authorities and commercial companies are able to undertake this. Clinical waste should be placed in yellow plastic bags, tied and labelled. These should then be placed in a secure locked container to await collection by the disposing authority.

Microbiological specimens

A letter to the *British Medical Journal* soon after the initiation of fundholding highlighted the possible consequences of primary care practitioners undertaking microbiological testing without adequate precautions to prevent contamination and cross infection[1].

It is perfectly feasible for any person to set up an incubator and to 'plate out' bacteriological swabs. However the dangers of ineffectual disposal of the specimens or culture plates are great. Any practitioner contemplating setting-up any kind of microbiology laboratory should ensure that he or she is able to work according to the guidelines issued by the Advisory Committee on Dangerous Pathogens[2].

Minor surgery and dentistry

Staff engaged in undertaking minor operative procedures in primary care should wear surgical gloves and single-use plastic aprons as a minimum. Face masks and eye protection are advisable to prevent the eyes and mucous membranes from blood splashes.

Legionnaire's disease

Legionnaire's disease is a form of pneumonia that principally affects those who have some degree of infirmity due to age, immunosuppression, smoking or other illness. Most cases have been attributed to water services in buildings or air conditioning systems.

In order to prevent the possibility of infection with *Legionella*, the water system within the primary care centre should ensure that:

• The hot water tank will be heated to at least 60°C for a minimum of one hour daily.

- The hot water distribution will achieve a temperature of 50°C within one minute of running the tap.
- Cold water will be stored below 20°C.

Staff are warned that the water at 50°C is hot and risk of scalding in the very young or old. Hence, caution should be used when washing hands.

The temperatures of the water should be checked twice a year by the safety officer or manager.

Contaminated instruments

Contaminated instruments should be cleaned and washed immediately after use according to the recommendations above. Any instruments left lying in sinks, or elsewhere, pose a risk to other patients and members of staff. It is the responsibility of the practitioner to ensure that all instruments are taken to the clinical preparation area, carried in a bucket or plastic outer container, and deposited in the disinfecting solution placed there for the purpose.

Instruments placed in sinks should be assumed to be infected and only handled when wearing latex or household rubber gloves.

Human immunodeficiency virus infection

The majority of procedures in primary care pose no risk of transmission of the HIV infection. The passage of HIV from health care practitioner to patient is negligible.

In order to avoid the passage of infection, good hygiene and procedures are necessary and the Expert Advisory Group on AIDS[3] have recommended that 'Health Care Workers who are either HIV or Hepatitis B antigen positive should not perform procedures where there is a risk that injury to the worker may result in the exposure of the patient's open tissues to the blood of the worker'. Such procedures would include contact with:

- Sharp instruments
- Needles
- Sharp tissues (e.g. spicules of bone)

Risk of injury and spread of infection is increased if the health care worker is working where he or she cannot visualise hands or fingertips (e.g. working in a body cavity).

Procedures where the hands and fingertips are visible and outside the patient's body at all times, together with internal examinations or procedures which do not require the use of sharp instruments (e.g. cervical cytology or proctoscopy, phlebotomy, minor skin suturing) are not considered to be exposure prone provided good practice guidelines are followed at all times.

If a health care worker is known to have HIV or another highly dangerous transmissible disease such as hepatitis, then he or she should seek specialist advice from his or her peers and employers.

The employer's responsibilities

The employer should maintain awareness of the necessary professional bodies' statements of ethical responsibilities and occupational guidance for AIDS and HIV. It may be worthwhile advising new staff of the requirement to sign a declaration and perhaps to offer routine confidential testing for staff likely to expose patients to risk.

If an employer is aware that an employee becomes a carrier of HIV or hepatitis, then utmost confidentiality should be maintained. That employee should be counselled appropriately and perhaps offered re-employment in another area of work which would not expose others to risk of infection.

The ethics regarding medical, dental or other professional practitioners working in partnership who contract HIV or hepatitis suggest that an approach should be made to the professional body for advice and assistance.

Clinical specimens

Phlebotomy

Bleeding patients carry a certain amount of risk. These risk areas are assessed as:

1 Needle injury to clinician before and after taking blood.
2 Contamination by blood leaking from specimen containers or syringe.
3 Fracture of specimen container.
4 Fainting or convulsing by the patient.

Good infection control measures[4]

Apply good basic hygiene practices with regular hand washing

Cover existing wounds or skin lesions with waterproof dressings

Avoid exposure-prone procedures if suffering from chronic skin lesions on hands

Avoid contamination of person by appropriate use of protective clothing

Protect mucous membrane of eyes, mouth and nose from blood splashes

Prevent puncture wounds, cuts and abrasions in the presence of blood

Avoid sharps usage wherever possible

Institute safe procedures for handling and disposal of needles and other sharps

Institute approved procedures for sterilisation and disinfection of instruments and equipment

Clear up spillages of blood and other body fluids promptly and disinfect surfaces

Institute a procedure for the safe disposal of contaminated waste

5   Infective disease transmission from the blood to the clinician in event of a needle injury or blood spillage.

There are risks to the patient:

1   Poor technique resulting in multiple puncture.
2   Fainting/convulsing following phlebotomy.
3   Bruising or failure to stop blood flow.
4   Tourniquets being left on limb.
5   Allergy to adhesive tapes used to bandage arm after venepuncture.

There are also risks to the laboratory workers when handling specimens.

Minimising risks

Good phlebotomy technique minimises risks to all parties. Taking blood requires preparation and assessment of the patient and provision of lying or sitting positions. The chance of fainting is smaller if the patient lies head down.

Students and other inexperienced staff should not undertake invasive procedures on patients who are known to be at risk of serious infection (HIV or hepatitis for example).

All necessary implements should be assembled prior to venepuncture. The site of venepuncture should be assessed first and tourniquets only used if essential.

The needle should not be handled by the patient or clinician before or after taking blood. The needle should be removed from the syringe using the appropriate aperture on the sharps box.

Gloves should be worn. Although this may seem unnecessary for many patients who might be assumed to be free of infection, they serve to protect the patient from the practitioner! Gloves must certainly be used when there are cuts or abrasions on the hands of the practitioner or if the patient is 'restless' or known to be infected and when handling the transfer of blood from syringe to sample bottles. The caps of the sample bottles should be securely screwed or inserted and the contents of the bottle mixed by simple inversion if appropriate.

Vacuum collection systems should be used as directed by the manufacturer and the barrels should not be re-used if the patient is of high risk or if there is blood contamination on the barrel. The barrel can only be re-used if the needle is removed. Removal of the needle is only advised if a specific needle-removing device is available – otherwise the needle and barrel assembly should be discarded.

The patient should be advised to press firmly on the venepuncture site with a pad of gauze or cotton wool for at least two minutes in order to stem the blood flow and to prevent bruising. The bleeding site should be inspected for a further minute to ensure there is no further bleeding.

If bandaging is necessary, simple cotton wool and synthetic adhesive tape is the most appropriate and the patient should be instructed to remove this on his/her return home and to report any further bleeding. The sample and appropriate forms should be labelled as below.

Other specimens

Examination and taking of specimens from patients requires good clinical technique. Not only is it important that diseases are not caught by the clinician, but it is equally important that the clinician does not pass to patients any infection that he or she might have. This is a particular problem with instruments which might be used to assist the examination process.

All instrument must be thoroughly cleaned and sterilised after use according to the recommendations above. If clean instruments are not available, then either disposable instruments should be used, or the patient requested to return when suitable instruments are available.

When examining the patient, latex gloves should be worn to prevent cross-infection. The gloves, once used, should be disposed of by placing in the yellow clinical waste sacs – they should **not** be placed in the ordinary paper waste bins.

When taking swabs from a patient, the swab should be inserted carefully into the culture medium without coming into contact with the clinician. Any contamination must be washed thoroughly with soap and running water.

Remember: Hepatitis can be caught easily from the body fluid of an infected patient.

Samples brought onto the premises by the patient

There are a number of types of specimen which the patient himself will bring onto the practice premises having completed the collection at home. This should cause no problem if the specimen bottle was labelled correctly by the practitioner before being given to the patient. It is best to instruct the patient carefully when suggesting the specimen and to provide a suitable container, request form and plastic bag(s).

If the patient brings a sample in an unsuitable or unlabelled container, he should be asked to transfer the specimen to another appropriately labelled container. Alternatively the original specimen provided by the patient should be placed in a labelled plastic bag by the patient himself before being placed in an outer bag by the practitioner.

On no account should reception staff be expected to receive bottles or specimens from patients without adequate outer protection. If this has to happen, then a supply of latex procedure gloves should be available for receptionists to wear before handling such specimens.

Labelling

Any specimen taken from a patient for laboratory analysis must be labelled with the name, date of birth and date of specimen as a minimum. Where possible, full labelling with address and a unique reference number (e.g. the NHS number) is preferable. The specimen should be placed in a plastic bag and sealed with the pathology request form, similarly labelled, attached.

All labels must be self-adhesive. **Labels must _never_ be licked.**

The person who sends the specimen must ensure that the container used is the appropriate one for the purpose, is properly closed, and is not externally contaminated by its contents. If the specimen is taken from a patient in whom any of the following diseases is suspected or known, then further labelling is essential as indicated:

- HIV
- Hepatitis B
- Mycobacterium tuberculosis (TB)
- Salmonella typhi

These specimens should be sent in individual sealed plastic bags within an outer plastic bag and clearly identified by a *yellow* **'Danger of infection'** label on both the request form and each specimen container. An extra label on the outside of the plastic bag is also helpful.

If the specimen is too large for a normal plastic specimen transit bag, then specimen containers should be enclosed in individual clear plastic sacks tied at the neck. The specimen form should be placed in a separate plastic envelope which is then securely tied at the neck of the sack.

Transport to the laboratory

Special secure transport carriers should be used to transport pathological and haematology specimens from the primary care centre to the laboratory. This carrier must be used correctly and must not be overfilled. If possible, all specimens must be kept upright.

The specimen transport boxes must not be used for any other purpose.

The specimen transport box will be cleaned and disinfected weekly or immediately after contamination.

Such boxes should contain any breakage and spillage and also be able to protect specimens from extremes of heat or cold. Many practices adapt 'picnic' cold food carriers which are sturdy and vacuum insulated.

Transport by post/messenger

Post Office regulations state that only first class letter post or datapost services may be used. Parcel post service may *not* be used.

Every pathological specimen must be enclosed in a primary container, hermetically sealed or otherwise securely closed. Except where otherwise specifically permitted, the capacity of the primary container must not exceed 50 ml (though multi-specimen packs may be approved). The primary container must be wrapped in sufficient absorbent material (e.g. cotton wool) to absorb all possible leakage in the event of damage, and sealed in a leakproof plastic bag.

The receptacle and its immediate packaging must then be placed in one of the following:

- A polypropylene clip-down container.
- A cylindrical light-metal container.
- A strong cardboard box with full length lid.
- The appropriate groove in a two-piece polystyrene box. Any empty spaces filled with absorbent material and the two parts of the box must then be firmly held together by self-adhesive plastic tape.

A padded bag is recommended as an outer cover. The outer cover or wrapping must be conspicuously labelled **'Pathological specimen – fragile with care'**. It must show the name and address of the sender to be contacted in case of damage or leakage.

Notes

1. Kibbler and Gillespie (1991) *British Medical Journal*, **302** (April), 851.
2. Advisory Committee on Dangerous Pathogens (1990) Categorisation of pathogens according to hazard and categories of containment (2nd edn). London, HMSO.
3. Expert Advisory Group on Aids can be contacted via secretariat: Department of Health, Room 727, Wellington House, 133–155 Waterloo Road, London. Tel: 0171 972 4349.
4. Expert Advisory Committee on AIDS (1990) Guidance for clinical health care workers: protection against infection with HIV and hepatitis virus — recommendations of the Expert Advisory Committee on AIDS. HMSO, January.

4

Drugs/diagnostic agents

The partners (or associates) should recognise that there are specific dangers in all medications stored on the practice premises. For the most part there should be no need for any member of staff other than clinical staff to handle medications, drugs, injections or similar chemicals.

The partners (or associates) and nurses who handle drugs should follow the routines advised to them in their training, being aware particularly of the following risks:

- Ampoules of injections often fracture when 'snapped open'. Hence the hand should be protected by wrapping the ampoule in a piece of clean cloth. Undue force should not be used to open an ampoule; if it does not open easily, it will require filing along the snap-mark.
- Some vials of injections create a positive pressure which causes contents to spray out when opened. When opening or removing contents of a vial, then the eyes should be protected.
- When pouring contents from bottles, gloves should be worn to prevent spillage over the hands.

In the unforeseen circumstance that any employee or any other person working on the premises has the need to handle bottles or packets of medication, then every effort should be made to ensure that the packaging remains sealed and the drugs are placed in such a site that they are not a risk to anyone else, particularly children, entering the premises.

If drugs or diagnostic agents are handed in to the primary care centre for disposal they should be dealt with in the following manner:

1 **Drugs in sealed bottles or in packets as dispensed by a pharmacist.** These drugs should be stored in the cupboard designated for that purpose, and the cupboard locked.
2 **Drugs loose in unlabelled bottles or other containers.** These drugs should be placed in a clinical waste 'sharps' bin for ultimate incineration.

3   **Liquid medications.** These should be washed down the toilet (not sink) in a heavy flow of water with the windows open to provide ventilation in case of fumes.
4   **Drugs delivered to the premises for patient use.** These must be logged into the drug log and should be stored in the appropriate cupboard. The patient should be made aware that the medication is available for collection.
5   **Injections/other drugs which must be kept cool.** These must be placed in their delivery carton/packet in the storage fridges.

All staff are advised *not* to handle loose medication. If a patient hands over loose tablets, an envelope should be given to the patient for him/her to place drugs inside it and for him/her to label and seal the envelope. The envelope should be sealed by stapling, *not* licking.

Carriage of chemicals on the premises

Staff needing to carry medications or diagnostic agents or any other chemical around the surgery premises should adhere to the following advice:

• Liquids, including cleaning fluids, should be carried in a plastic bucket or similar container.
• Ampoules of injection should be carried only within their outer packaging of cardboard.
• Bottles or boxes of medications should be carried upright.

> No chemical or drug packet/box should be left in any public area at any time. No chemical or drug, whether in a packet or box, should be stored at a place accessible by a child.

Spillage of drugs or chemicals

The specific dangers are of personal contamination by physical contact, inhalation of fumes, injury to eyes, or injury by broken glass. If anything is dropped, broken or spilt, the area must be initially secured by asking for the assistance of another member of staff to keep guard while one person obtains the necessary equipment to clear the area. The person cleaning the area *must* wear gloves, and if appropriate an apron and eye protection. Glass should be swept into a dustpan and the area either wet-mopped and/or vacuumed immediately afterwards to remove any remaining splinters of glass.

Powders should be vacuumed and then wet mopped if flooring is suitable.

Liquids should be mopped using cold water. **No cleaning agents should be used.** The area should then be rinsed with clean water.

Drug/equipment administration

The 1987 Consumer Protection Act requires a producer to ensure that a product is up to standard and fit for the intended purpose. The supplier of any product has a responsibility to identify the producer when any damage is caused by a defect in the product. Failure to be able to identify the producer will result in liability resting with the supplier.

To ensure the health and safety of patients of the practice, it is essential that all drugs or items personally administered to any patient are appropriate, have not passed their expiry date, that the producer can be identified and that this information is properly recorded.

A suggested minimum record system is one in which there is a controlled record kept of:

- Drugs and equipment ordered.
- Delivery notes confirmed and signed.
- Entry into a drug/equipment log book with date of receipt, supplier's name, batch number and quantity received.
- A dispensing/supply log indicating patient's name, drugs/ equipment and quantities supplied, together with date, name of 'dispenser' and batch numbers.
- In the patient record – a note of the drug/equipment supplied together with name of manufacturer or supplier and batch number.

Such controlled records regrettably need to be kept for 15 years.

5

Basic life support

Sudden collapse

Sudden collapse can result in death if resuscitation is delayed. Resuscitation should be started immediately when there is sudden loss of consciousness and absent breathing and pulses. Cardiac arrests, particularly in younger people, can be a result of causes other than heart disease - e.g.: asthma, drugs, electrocution.

It is proposed as part of the policy of the primary care centre that all staff members should be trained in resuscitation techniques and that they should be prepared to use them in the event of collapse of a member of staff, patient or other member of public.

Basic life support should centre around:

1 Assessment of situation, and removal of the collapsed person from an area of risk (particularly when electrocution has occurred).
2 To ensure that the patient and person attending are also protected from outside risks (particularly road traffic if outside the premises).
3 Calling for assistance, including calling for an ambulance.
4 Maintaining the airway.
5 Initiating artificial respiration.
6 Maintaining the circulation.

Remember:	A... Airway	B... Breathing	C... Circulation

How to do it

1 **Assessment:** Make sure the area is safe. Ensure that there are no immediate dangers – live electrical apparatus, falling

machinery, spilt solvents. If electrical risk is present, use a broom handle or a rolled-up magazine/newspaper to isolate the patient from the mains. Disconnect any hazardous electrical apparatus from the mains if possible. If a there is smoke or gas hazard, remove the patient and yourself rapidly from the area of risk before attempting to resuscitate as you might collapse yourself.

Determine whether the 'patient' is unresponsive by careful shaking and asking the patient if he/she is able to hear you.

2 **Call for assistance:** Ask another person to dial 999 and request an ambulance for presumed cardiac arrest. Give location and telephone number. The other person should also alert any medical member of staff on duty who may be able to administer further assistance.

If no other member of staff or public is available, proceed to Step 3, meanwhile shouting for help.

3 **Open the airway:** The attendant should open the airway of the collapsed person by tilting the head backwards and elevating the chin. This will lift the tongue from the back of the throat. Any obstruction, such as *loose* dentures should be removed by hooking them out.

4 **Assisting breathing:** The patient should be observed for breathing by watching the chest or abdomen for movements; listening for breathing and feeling for expired air on the back of the hand. If there is no evidence of spontaneous breathing, then artificial respiration should be started.

If possible, use a barrier device to prevent direct mouth-to-mouth contact. Such a device should be available on the premises and all staff shown where it is kept. Otherwise a plastic bag with a hole punched through it can act as a barrier to transfer of any infection. **All members of staff should familiarise themselves with the Brook Airway or Laerdal Pocket Mask and its use**.

The Brook Airway is kept ...

Mouth-to-mouth resuscitation is recommended and should be given straight away. Two slow expired breaths of air should be given by the attendant to the patient, each sufficient to cause the chest to rise and fall between breaths. Each of the initial breaths should last from one to one and a half seconds.

Further breaths should be long enough to allow the chest to rise.

5 **Assisting circulation:** The patient's pulse should be felt in the neck – the carotid pulse should be palpated either side of the windpipe for at least five seconds before being sure that the circulation has stopped.

External cardiac massage should be learned using training mannequins. If training has not been received, then the attendant should give a single firm blow using a closed fist to the patient's chest. The pulse should then be re-checked. If resuscitation is still required, and no other trained person is present, then external cardiac massage should be begun by pressing firmly and rhythmically using the heel of the hand pressed into the patient's central sternum by the pressure of the attendant's other hand. This should be repeated up to 80 times a minute but interspersed with mouth-to-mouth breathing in the ratio of 15 compressions of the chest followed by two slow breaths.

The recovery position

If you have been successful in initiating respiration, then the patient should be checked for physical injury before being turned to the recovery position. This prevents the tongue rolling back to occlude the air passages and also prevents choking. There is no definitive position, but the following rules should apply:

1   The patient should be made safe so that he is not likely to fall or damage himself further.
2   The patient's head, neck and trunk should be kept in a straight line.
3   The position should permit gravity drainage of fluid from the patient's mouth, i.e. mouth lower than stomach and to one side.
4   Particular care should be exercised if there is any possibility of head injury or spinal injury. In these circumstances, the patient should only be moved using at least three other persons and the head and spine should be kept absolutely rigid in a straight line.

Choking

A conscious choking patient should be bent forward – for example, over a chair back – and encouraged to cough. If coughing fails to dislodge the blockage, then firm blows should be administered to the middle of the upper back. A trained first-aider should also administer abdominal thrusts (Heimlich manoeuvre). Alternating back blows and abdominal thrusts is the most effective measure.

An unconscious person should be given abdominal or chest thrusts by direct compression.

Faints

Fainting is common in a medical environment, usually by patients rather than by staff. If a person collapses from a faint, breathing and circulation are still intact, although a pulse at the wrist may feel weak, hence the neck pulses should be felt.

The patient should be laid on the floor (not a couch) in a position which follows the recovery rules outlined above. Tight clothing, particularly around the neck, should be loosened and help summoned. There should be no need to call for an ambulance if the cause is clear, but any medically trained person on site should be called for advice.

Recovery will usually be rapid but the patient should be encouraged to stay lying on the floor for some minutes before being slowly asked to sit. When the patient can sit comfortably, then they should be permitted to rise to an armchair. The patient should not be allowed to proceed out of the premises unaccompanied for at least 30 minutes after a faint. During this time they should sit somewhere under full observation. A medical check of blood pressure and breathing should be undertaken, if possible, by a doctor or nurse before the patient departs.

Epileptic convulsion

Patients and staff may experience an epileptic convulsion whilst at work. Convulsions may be full convulsions in which the patient shakes uncontrollably – often all limbs are affected – or may be mild convulsions which might go unnoticed by those around. Sometimes, the person becomes incontinent during a convulsion. Often the convulsion may be followed by a period of unconsciousness or heavy sleep.

For the most part, the patient should be left alone during a convulsion unless they are in a position whereby they might injure themselves further. If this is the case, then they should be carefully assisted to the floor and made comfortable there.

A member of staff should be allocated to maintain full observation of the patient and to ensure privacy from other patients if possible. When the patient recovers, he or she should be offered appropriate facilities to change if necessary and offered a medical check.

Only if the patient has never suffered a convulsion before should an ambulance be offered, or if the patient has caused himself harm through the convulsion. A medically trained person should be advised at the earliest possible opportunity.

Resuscitation equipment

The following minimum resuscitation equipment should be maintained on site:

Centrally or in a nursing station
- Oxygen
- Nebuliser
- Brook Airway or Laerdal Pocket Mask
- Drugs for anaphylactic shock
  - Adrenalin
  - Chlorpheniramine
  - Hydrocortisone
  - Atropine
- Adult and child airways

All consulting rooms
- Drugs for anaphylactic shock
  - Adrenalin
  - Chlorpheniramine
  - Hydrocortisone
  - Atropine
- Adult and child airways

6

Prevention of injury

Contaminated sharps injury

Practitioners working in or from the premises are at risk of injury from needles or glass ampoules of drugs. Although good clinical practice should avoid the risk of injury – and prevention is better than cure – it is inevitable that injury will arise periodically from a 'sharp'.

If an accidental injury arises from a sharp, then the following should be undertaken.

1 **Injury arising from personal injury with a contaminated needle following the taking of blood from a patient or from injecting a patient with a drug.** Every such injury should assume that the patient is contaminated with hepatitis or HIV. Hence the area must be washed thoroughly with water and soap and the sharps disposed of in a suitable secure container. The injury should be recorded in the accident book. The injured person should have his/her own blood checked for antibodies to hepatitis and HIV at six weeks and six months after the injury.

2 **An injury arising from self-inoculation with a needle or fragment of glass from an ampoule prior to giving an injection to the patient.** If the injury has arisen from the needle which is about to be used to give the injection, then that needle should be discarded safely in a sharps container and the area of injury thoroughly washed.

   If the injury has arisen from an ampoule, then the area should be washed and explored for glass fragments. Any fragments of glass on the floor or desk should be removed by brushing with paper or a brush onto a firm object such as a dustpan prior to being discarded in a sharps bin. The injury should be recorded without delay in the practice accident book. The wound should be covered with a waterproof dressing.

Management of exposure to hepatitis B virus

If a member of staff or a patient is exposed, through accidental self-inoculation or otherwise, to body fluid from a patient known to be infected with Hepatitis B (or one who is subsequently found to be infected), then the following course of action is suggested:

1   Wash the wound/puncture site well with soap and water, ensuring any needle or foreign body is removed. The wound should be inspected and then bandaged using an antiseptic and appropriate dressing.

2   If the employee or practitioner has not been fully immunised against hepatitis B, then arrangements should be made to obtain hepatitis B immunoglobulin from the local public health laboratory (in Scotland contact the Blood Transfusion Service[1]; in Northern Ireland, contact the Regional Virus Laboratory, Royal Victoria Hospital, Belfast, 01232 240503) who will also be able to give the latest advice on management of exposure to hepatitis.

Hepatitis B immunoglobulin is available in 2 ml ampoules containing 200 Iu and 5 ml ampoules containing 500 Iu.

Dosage: 0–4 yrs   200 iu im
          5–9 yrs   300 iu im
          10 yrs upwards   500 iu im

The practitioner should also be given a dose of hepatitis B vaccine and arrangements made to complete the course if a course of vaccination has not already been started.

3   If the employee or practitioner has been fully immunised against hepatitis B, then a booster dose of vaccine should be given unless they are known to have adequate levels of protective antibodies (over 100 miu/ml within the last two years).

If the patient is not hepatitis positive, then a non-immune member of staff should be given an immediate first dose of hepatitis B vaccine and arrangements made to continue the course in order to encourage protection prior to any subsequent injury.

Management of exposure to HIV

If patient is HIV negative: no action necessary.

If patient is believed to be at risk of HIV: the patient and the health care worker should be retested for HIV after three to six months. The health care worker should have a sample of blood stored for possible future HIV antibody testing (for a baseline estimation).

If the patient is known to be HIV positive: then arrangements should be made for the staff member to receive expert counselling (usually from a local HIV specialist team) and for a baseline blood sample to be stored for future antibody testing. If there is significant risk of the staff member receiving a blood inoculation from the patient – for example a deep wound or needlestick injury – then the local specialist HIV team should be contacted for advice which may include the recommendation of prophylaxis with zidovudine. This will need to be administered within 24 hours of the injury.

The affected staff member should also be advised to take immediate steps to prevent further transmission by not donating blood and by using barrier contraception.

Further blood testing should be undertaken at three to six monthly intervals to ensure that HIV infection has not occurred.

Waste disposal procedure (part of COSHH assessment)

The premises are required to be registered under Duty of Care Regulations for the safe disposal of any waste it generates. The appointed collector/receiver of waste is identified under each specific waste category below.

The Duty of Care Regulations are part of the Environmental Protection Act which ensures that wastes are stored, treated, transported and disposed of in any way to maximise the protection of the environment. Any waste produced from any business, industrial or commercial premises, is defined as controlled waste.

Contaminated sharps

On-site storage

- In plastic containers coloured yellow and white with secure fittings and which can safely sealed without coming into contact with contents. Containers to comply with BS7320.
- These containers are known as 'sharps bins' and must always be kept above child height.

- These containers should not be overfilled to the extent that they do not automatically self-seal.
- No attempt should ever be made to insert fingers into the sharps bin.

Clinical waste

On-site storage

- All clinical waste, including any material which has come into contact with bodily fluid other than sharps, as defined above, is deposited in yellow clinical waste sacks. These sacks are tied firmly at the neck and a descriptive label attached. Such sacks are then placed in a secure lockable store.

Notes

1 Aberdeen 01224 681818; Dundee 01382 645166; Edinburgh 0131 2297291; Glasgow 01698 373315/8; Inverness 01463 234151.

7

The work environment

The work environment is one that is constantly changing as practitioners and members of staff take on new responsibilities and when new methods of working are agreed. It is essential that responsibility for the welfare of everyone working in the primary care premises is considered otherwise there will be cost not only in decreased work efficiency, but possibly in compensation for injury. Recent cases involving repetitive strain injury have resulted in considerable damages being awarded.

This section aims to cover the various changes in recommendations for good working practice within the EC. It should form the basis for any practice policy.

Visual display units

The practitioners or associates should recognise that increasing use is being made of computers and related equipment which involves VDUs. Although many of the employees of the practice use the VDU displays for short periods of time only, others, particularly on the management and secretarial side of the practice may sit for long periods of time at a VDU. The following recommendations apply to all users irrespective of the length of time that they sit working continuously at a VDU. The recommendations also apply to the partners, associates and other medical staff.

Equipment

Equipment should have been selected to provide the least risk to the user in terms of glare and flicker. The recommendations of the Health and Safety Executive regarding new equipment need to be taken into account when any further equipment is purchased or existing equipment modified.

All equipment needs to be maintained and cleaned on a regular basis according to the schedule defined in the practice technical manual[1].

All VDU monitors should have tip and tilt rotation mechanisms to allow the user to select the most appropriate position. The monitors used for secretarial and management purposes should also have facilities to raise and lower the monitor. Each monitor should be fitted with a screen to decrease glare. The monitor will be adjustable for brightness and contrast. All monitors will emit negligible radiation.

The keyboard needs to be separate from the computer and monitor and shall be tiltable so as to allow the operator to find a comfortable position. There shall be space in front of the keyboard for siting a support for the operator's wrists/forearm. All regular users of keyboards should be offered (and this recorded in the employee record) an adjustable wrist support and shown its correct usage in order to prevent repetitive strain injury.

The working area

- A chair needs to be provided for each computer/VDU site. This chair should be fully adjustable and stable. It will be easily adjusted to provide back support, height variation and rake of back support.
- A foot-rest should be provided for those sites where prolonged usage of the computer terminal is necessary.
- There should be appropriate background and local lighting.
- Document holders should be provided where individual assessment reveals that they would be of use.
- Ambient noise levels need to be reduced as much as possible within the limits of technology available. Printers will be muffled if feasible.

Computer software/tasks

It is imperative that adequate training be given to all staff in order that they may use the appropriate software in the most economical manner. All software should be appropriate to the tasks required of it and choice will always be made taking into account the needs of the users.

Daily work routine

VDU workers should also follow the advice given in the section below on repetitive strain injuries.

In general, the following guidance should be followed by regular users of VDUs and keyboards.

1   Breaks should be taken before the onset of fatigue – not in order to recuperate.
2   Breaks should be taken when performance is maximum, rather than when productivity reduces.
3   A break is one which uses different visual inputs and different arm actions – it is not necessarily a rest break.
4   Breaks or changes of activity are included in working time. They should reduce the workload at the screen.
5   Short, frequent breaks are more satisfactory than occasional longer breaks and these should be taken away from the screen. Informal breaks – time not spent viewing the screen (e.g. in consultation with a patient) appear from study evidence to be more effective in relieving visual fatigue than formal rest breaks.

The practitioners or their manager will advise the most appropriate manner of work in order that breaks or changes of activity are taken by users during their normal work. However, discretion is left to the employee to allow the optimal distribution of effort over the working day.

Eyes and eyesight

All employees who use a VDU are entitled to request an appropriate eye or eyesight test which will be carried out by a competent person which may be a medical or ophthalmic practitioner who may work within the practice. This test will include distant and near vision testing and also colour testing. Eye testing cannot be carried out against the will of the employee.

If the eye testing reveals any abnormality, then the employee will be asked to undergo appropriate further testing. The employer will not be responsible for any corrective prescriptions for eye complaints which are not related to display screen work. The employer will, however, pay for specific and 'special' corrective appliances of a basic quality necessary for the continuation of the employee's work. It remains the prerogative of the employer to specify the optometrist/optician requested to assess and provide such corrective appliances.

Repeat eyesight testing will be undertaken at appropriate intervals depending upon the individual's specific tasks and general health. Repeat eyesight testing will be undertaken at the request of the employee.

Avoidance of repetitive strain injury

Repetitive strain injury includes such problems as 'tennis elbow or golfer's elbow'. It is an inflammation of a tendon or group of tendons around a joint. Repetitive action can cause an increase in size of the tendons resulting in pain, numbness, weakness and spasm.

The injury is becoming increasingly recognised in those people who are working in offices, particularly where technology has changed and different strains are being placed on the body. Using word processors or computers, for example, requires little physical force to depress the keys, compared to typewriters, and hence typing can often become faster, putting extra strain on the joints which are often held in a single position for long periods of time. Other jobs also cause RSI.

Although treatment of RSI is becoming increasingly available, avoidance is preferred. If you are working in an office, you should try to do the following:

*   Adopt a comfortable posture when seated. Sit back in your chair so that the back is supported firmly. You should not lean forward to work. At all times the chair should give you some lumbar support.
*   Relax your shoulders and keep your wrists balanced – if using a keyboard for long periods of time, make use of a wrist support in front of the keyboard.
*   Avoid sitting still for too long. Periodically move your arms, legs, shoulders and neck.
*   Plan your work carefully in order to allow for mental and physical variation.
*   When appropriate, make best use of document holders, telephone headsets, etc., in order to minimise strains.
*   Take short, but regular breaks if confined to a single task for a long period of time.

Working conditions

Ventilation

The premises are best constructed to allow windows and doors to be opened easily to accommodate a range of climatic conditions. Ventilation can then be adjusted to meet personal requirements. Any enclosed room should have an electrical fan which can be operated to aid circulation of air and portable fans may otherwise be made available as required.

Temperature

Central heating and ventilation can be adjusted to provide a comfortable working environment for all staff. The temperature of the offices should be at least 16°C after the first working hour of each day. If temperatures fall below this, then local portable heaters need to be made available. If the temperature rises too high, then increased ventilation should be used to decrease the room temperature and the heating should be switched off.

Any difficulties in the temperature control of the building should be reported to the Safety Liaison Officer. A thermometer should be sited in the main office to monitor room temperature. The central heating system will be serviced annually by contract and any faults repaired immediately.

Lighting

Ceiling lights are available in each room and local lights can be provided which are adjusted so as to best illuminate particular work. The public areas and corridors ought to remain lit throughout the working day unless the natural light is sufficiently bright. External lighting of porch and steps will be required from dusk to dawn. The interior of the light units will be cleaned monthly or more often as required and the practice maintenance officer will repair any defective lights if reported to him via the maintenance book.

Emergency lighting

Battery powered emergency lights need to be situated in the public corridors and their functioning should be checked at least twice a year.

Room dimensions

The practice should comply with the recommendation that each member of staff will have a minimum of 11 cubic metres of space when working in a room, apart from times of group meetings when, for short periods, more people than usual are sitting in one room.

All rooms will need to be designed to allow the most appropriate movement between workstations without encroaching on other workers' personal space.

Flooring

The flooring within the premises needs to be designed to minimise wear and tear in the areas where patients pass most frequently – the entrance lobby and the waiting room. The main parts of the building, however, should perhaps be carpeted for comfort and for noise reduction. The clinical room(s) should have a sealed hard surface for hygiene purposes.

Flooring will need to be cleaned daily in the public areas and at least twice a week in all other areas. Floors should be kept free of obstructions which may present a hazard or impede access. If a hazard is encountered, all members of staff have a duty to try to rectify the hazard, or to make everyone else aware of the situation. If the floor is damaged, it should be notified immediately to the practice maintenance officer and the area protected until such time that it is repaired.

External surfaces will be brushed daily to remove possible environmental hazards and gritted/salted if necessary to prevent icing. Handrails should be provided either side of the slopes and steps.

Accommodation for personal belongings

It is necessary to make hanging space for outdoor clothes available on the premises and access to this will be by a key given to each member of staff. Valuable items of personal possession should not be brought to the premises except at the owner's own liability. However, lockable drawers and cupboards can be made available for storing such items.

Smoking

Smoking on any part of the premises is *not allowed* either by staff, partners, or patients. Any patient entering the premises smoking will be asked to leave the premises until his/her cigarette is finished, or until he/she extinguishes the cigarette/cigar/pipe.

First aid boxes

First aid box(es) need to be kept on the premises and equipped to the Factories Act Standard. These will be checked weekly by the practice nurse or safety officer and any items missing will be replaced immediately.

The first aid box is marked by a square green sticker with a white cross.

The First Aid boxes are sited at:

Suitable contents for a first aid box:
- One guidance card
- 20 individually wrapped sterile adhesive dressings or assorted sizes
- Two sterile eye pads
- Six individually wrapped triangular bandages
- Six safety pins
- Six medium sized individually wrapped plain wound dressings
- Two large individually wrapped plain wound dressings
- Three extra-large individually wrapped plain wound dressings
- Eye wash, sterile
- Scissors
- Forceps for removal of foreign objects such as glass

Nominated first aid officers

At least one member of staff should undergo a recognised 'First Aid at Work' course organised by the British Red Cross. All regular members of staff need also to be encouraged to undergo some formal first aid training in the early years of their employment.

Accident book

Provision
A bound hardback book has to be provided by the practice for the purpose of recording all untoward happenings and will be kept in a central place – perhaps adjacent to the first aid box found in the premises. This book will be used for the sole purpose of recording accidents happening on the premises to staff, partners or patients. It will also be used to record any accidents or untoward events occurring to members of staff or partners/associates when on practice business off the practice premises.

Recording
The accident book will record the date, the place, the circumstances, the name, sex and occupation of the injured person and the nature of the injury.

Any dangerous occurrence, such as the overheating of an autoclave, or an explosion from a piece of electrical equipment or any major incident resulting in the fracture of a bone or the loss of any part of a limb or sight, will be reported to the Health and Safety Executive on form F2508[2] within 72 hours of the occurrence. All records will be kept for a minimum of three years.

Electrical equipment

The Electricity at Work Regulations 1989 require employers to protect users of portable electrical appliances from electric shock and fire. This is best undertaken on the premises by a regular programme of inspection, testing and recording for every piece of electrical equipment.

Equipment covered by this regulation includes all appliances with plug and flex. This includes extension leads, VDUs, kettles, electric tills, photocopiers, fax machine, video players, portable heaters, fridges, dictation equipment and answerphones, to name but a few.

An approved contractor should be asked to undertake testing of all portable electrical appliances at least annually and will record the results of such tests in a log kept specifically for the purpose. This log is a controlled document and can be inspected at any time by the Health and Safety Executive. The contractor will either be a member of the National Inspection Council for Electrical Installation Contracting or a member of the Electrical Contractors Association.

The minimum check will include:

- Visual inspection for signs of damage or deterioration of casing, cable sheath, plugs and terminals.
- Examine the plug for fuse of correct rating.
- Check polarity of connections.
- Earth continuity test which consists of a substantial test current (typically 25A) from the plug earth to any exposed metalwork on the appliance. Class 2 (double insulated) appliances are subject to a flash test.
- Insulation test, which consists of the application of a test voltage (typically 500 V DC for 240 V AC equipment) between live, neutral and earth.

Some equipment, particularly computer equipment, may be damaged by application of a high test voltage or current. In such circumstances, the tests above may be limited and will be recorded as such.

Each piece of equipment will be logged separately and identified by a serial number.

Gas appliances

Some 40 people die in the UK annually from carbon monoxide poisoning caused by faulty or poorly installed gas appliances[3]. Gas appliances should be installed by a registered gas installer (CORGI in the UK). All gas appliances need air to work safely and therefore require adequate ventilation.

A weekly check of all gas appliances should be made checking:

- That their ventilation is not obstructed internally or externally.
- The gas flue will also be checked to ensure that waste gases can escape.
- The appliance itself should be checked for undue wear:
  - Staining, sooting or discoloration on the appliance or surrounding decorations;
  - A yellow or orange flame instead of the normal blue;
  - A strange smell when the gas appliance is working.

An annual service of the gas appliance should be undertaken by a CORGI-registered installer.

Notes

1 If a technical manual does not exist you are encouraged to create one. This will list all items of electrical and technical equipment in use in the practice. It should include a copy of operating instructions, warranties and servicing arrangements. Any new members of staff who require to use equipment in their work (anything from a vacuum cleaner to a dental drill) should be given training based on the information recorded in the technical manual
2 Obtainable from the Health and Safety Executive
3 British Gas statistics

8

Fire precautions

Fire procedure

The Fire Precautions Act of 1971 requires that premises that are used as a place of work by more than 20 persons at the same time are assessed and inspected by the local fire authority. This inspection will determine that the premises are reasonably equipped with a means of escape, of fighting a fire and **of giving warning of a fire**.

Even if fewer than 20 persons are employed, the Fire Precautions (Non-Certified Factory, Office, Shop and Railway Premises) Regulations 1976 will apply. These require:

1 The doors through which a worker might have to pass to get out must not be locked or fastened such that they cannot be easily and immediately opened on the way out; and

2 The contents of the workroom should be so arranged as to afford free passageway to a means of escape in case of fire; and

3 There shall be provided and maintained appropriate means of fighting fire placed readily available for use.

The policy of the practice needs to be to comply with all these appropriate regulations such that the fire precautions will be assessed regularly at least every six months.

Advice should be sought of the fire brigade or similar consultant as to the fire extinguishing needs of the premises in order that extinguishers for all types of fire will be provided and all staff trained in their proper usage. It is recognised that the following types of extinguisher will be needed

• Powder/foam: For paper and material fires.
• CO_2: For electrical fires.

Fire exit doors will need to be clearly marked and a means of evacuation of the premises will have to be displayed in each work area.

Fire bells and alarms should be tested for electrical function every week and a fire practice will be held at least every three months to ensure compliance with the fire evacuation procedure.

As with all health and safety issues, prevention is better than cure. Hence all staff should be asked to do their best to identify and report to the safety officer or a member of the management team all possible sources of fire. The management team will identify means of preventing such sources from resulting in fire.

Fire evacuation procedure

In the event of a fire requiring emergency evacuation of the premises, the main aims are to:

1   Activate the alarm at the main entrance to the building and to telephone the fire brigade.
2   Evacuate all patients and staff through the safest exit point.
3   Practitioner(s) present to check that all rooms are empty and to close doors behind them.
4   Not re-enter the building without advice from the fire brigade.
5   Alert residents in adjacent buildings of a fire risk.

Points to remember

In the event of a fire the person finding the fire should, if feasible, attempt to put it out using one of the practice's extinguishers.

- The **black** extinguisher (CO2) to be used for **electrical fires.**
- The large **white** extinguisher (foam) should be used for *any other kind of fire.*
- The **red** extinguisher (water) should be used for **paper or fabric fires.**

If the fire is not easily and quickly extinguished then this person should be responsible for alerting other members of staff, practitioners and patients to the danger and should activate the alarm at the nearest point.

The **senior staff member** present in the building, or the switchboard operator should be responsible for telephoning the fire brigade. The **senior practitioner** present should also be alerted by this staff member.

The **senior practitioner** present should be responsible for ensuring the orderly evacuation of the premises. He/she should also check the rooms carefully to ensure full evacuation and that all doors are closed.

The **senior staff member** will delegate to another staff member the task of alerting other residents and occupants of adjacent buildings.

All patients and staff must be evacuated to the muster point.

The muster point is: _____

The **senior practitioner** present will take a roll call of staff and other attached personnel. All evacuated persons will stay at the muster point until advised by the fire officer that the premises are safe.

Fire extinguishers are located at:

9

Manual handling procedures

Patients – lifting

Many accidents happen to staff in health care environments through lifting or manoeuvring patients. This risk is very much less in primary care, as for the most part patients are ambulant to attend the practice. However, risks do occur for practice staff who attend a patient's home and when a patient falls or collapses on the practice premises.

Patients – falling or collapsing whilst on practice premises

On no account must any attempt be made to lift the patient without a medical assessment being first made in the case of fractured limbs. If a medical assessment indicates that it is safe for the patient to try to stand, then the patient should be first encouraged to try to stand unaided – this may be helped by the patient turning onto their front, pushing upwards with their arms to a sitting or kneeling position, then holding onto a chair to assist climbing to a vertical position. If assistance is necessary, then two other persons must assist, one on each side of the patient. If two persons are not available and help cannot be obtained from another source, then the patient can be assisted by linking their arms around your neck, your hands linked behind their back, and the patient brought up to a vertical position. The patient should not be released until you have checked that balance is firm.

Patients – falling at home

If a patient calls stating that they have fallen and cannot rise, then an ambulance should be requested. Ambulance officers are trained in lifting patients and they also have equipment to assist.

If a visiting clinician finds a patient on the floor at home, then a medical assessment should be made. If this assessment reveals no fractured bones, then an immediate assessment should be made of the feasibility of the patient standing themselves or with minimal assistance. If the latter is not possible, then help should be summoned and the patient protected from harm. Cover with a blanket or other warm object.

Patients who have a suspected fracture, or pain on standing, should be referred for investigation at the hospital casualty unit without delay.

Boxes

Inanimate objects such as boxes or filing cabinets can cause more damage to someone lifting them than can a collapsed patient. Items delivered to the practice should be placed, by the delivery agent, as near as possible to their ultimate destination – particularly items of furniture or equipment. Boxes of goods should not be moved by lifting. Unpacking and checking of contents should be undertaken at the point of delivery to the practice.

If an object is to be lifted, the operator should lift with a straight back and with his/her knees together. If the object is difficult or heavy, then two or more people should lift it in a coordinated manner. Any injury occurring as a result of lifting should be recorded fully in the practice accident book.

Bags of waste

Bags of waste present a lifting hazard. Often these are not particularly heavy, but the act of disposing of the full bag will require a twisting and lifting action which is potentially damaging to the spinal joint. If a waste bag is to be lifted into a dustbin or secure repository, then it should be done with a straight back and without twisting the spine. It is better to move physically in an arc than to twist the spine whilst lifting. If appropriate, assistance should be requested.

Noxious substances

Eye protection

Carrying or lifting any form of chemical must be undertaken with great caution. Consideration must be given to the effect of dropping and breaking the container. Hence operators are advised never to carry a container of chemical directly; it should be carried in a waterproof outer container which would contain any spilt chemicals. Eye and clothing protection should be worn in such circumstances and another person alerted to watch over the procedure in order to call for help if an accident should happen. Noxious substances should not be moved around the practice premises when members of the public are present.

10

Personal risk assessment: general principles

Practice nurses and medical practitioners

All clinical members of staff are at risk from a wide variety of hazards. Without repeating the whole of this document, the tasks undertaken by clinical members of staff and the partners of the practice fall into all categories mentioned here.

Particular risks are those of self-injection of drugs; accidental self-injection with contaminated sharps; and personal attack by patients on or off the premises.

Management of these risks requires constant awareness of the environment in which the clinician is practising and a constant desire to ensure that such an environment is safe for both practitioner and patient.

Health visitors and community workers

Community health visiting staff utilising the facilities of the practice must be aware of all the risks present which have been covered by this document.

As health visitors will often be dealing with very young children who all have very enquiring minds, it is imperative that they ensure that all possible sources of danger are removed from the climbing range of toddlers and their older siblings. Ingestion of chemicals and damage by sharps are essential to avoid.

Personal risk is less than with clinicians, but the potential is present and all staff using the premises should be signatories to having read and understood the practice's health and safety policy document.

When attending the premises for the purposes of holding a child clinic, the health visitor should inspect the clinic room(s) for possible child hazards and correct such hazards, or report such to the safety liaison officer. No clinic should start until such time that all hazards have been cleared.

Practice receptionists

Practice reception staff undertake a wide range of duties: some involving spending time at a VDU; some in repetitive telephone work; some in dealing with deliveries of goods to the premises and some in patient contact. At the same time, they are required to respond to calls from the practitioners and to keep an overview of the building.

VDU risk assessment is available to all reception staff although it is not expected that they will ever spend long uninterrupted periods operating a VDU.

Risk of personal attack is present and reception staff should be aware of the practice procedures for calling for assistance and avoiding personal risk.

Verbal telephone abuse is a risk to the mental health of the receptionist. Training in telephone technique needs to be given to all receptionists as part of their induction course.

Caution in lifting objects and patients – reference is made to Chapter 9, Manual handling procedures.

Practice secretarial staff

Secretarial staff are at risk of repetitive strain injury and other physical injuries from repeated actions at word processors/ computers. All such management and secretarial staff should take note of the recommendations present in this guide in Chapter 7, The work environment. Wrist supports, adjustable seating, adjustable VDU monitors and foot rests need to be provided for the use of all such staff. Frequent visual breaks away from the monitors should be taken. Eye assessments are provided free of charge to such employees. These eye assessments will be arranged by the safety liaison officer at the request of the member of staff and suitable corrective aids will be provided if deemed necessary.

Practice housekeeping staff

Housekeeping staff are at high risk of self-injury and infection from sharps and specimens in clinical areas.

Provision of protective gloves is an essential requirement of the employer, as are protective safety spectacles.

Attention should be paid to the section in Chapter 9 on disposal of clinical and non-clinical waste; the section in Chapter 11 on

COSHH; the sections in Chapter 3 on hazards from body fluids and Chapter 12 on cleaning of the practice premises.

All housekeeping staff need to be offered immunisation at practice cost against hepatitis and other communicable diseases.

To decrease risk to other users of the premises, the housekeeping staff should ensure that hazard warning signs are displayed during cleaning.

Practice maintenance staff

Injury from use of machines, electric shock and falling are particular risks for the practice maintenance staff. As with cleaning staff, protective gloves are an essential provision, as are protective safety spectacles.

When using ladders, the employee is advised to ensure that the ladder is correctly assembled and any safety latches fastened. Tools and equipment used by maintenance staff pose a risk to other employees. Such equipment should be carefully placed away from possible contact with other members of staff or members of the public.

If access to a particular part of the premises is not possible easily and safely, then specialist access equipment will need to be hired, or an outside contractor employed to undertake the work. Whenever possible, maintenance should only be undertaken when the practice is closed to the general public and when another person can be present to give assistance.

Personal attack

Policy in dealing with violence

All members of staff are at risk of attack from patients and regrettably the incidence of physical abuse aimed at health care practitioners and their staff is increasing. It is therefore imperative that practitioners and staff avoid confrontation which might lead to physical abuse.

It is important to understand that any patient (even those who appear placid) can become so enraged that they become dangerous. Some types of mental illness result in a rapid swing between docility and aggression. It is not always the obstreperous drunk who causes the most harm.

- A panic button should be installed at the main reception desk which is connected to the main practice alarm. All reception staff should ensure that they understand how to operate this device.
- Each consulting room should be equipped with an alarm button which, when activated, signals to other persons in the building that help is required.
- Upon hearing any alarm, all other practitioners should attend the appropriate room and the senior receptionist present should be prepared to summon the police.
- It is worth considering the arrangement of the seating in the waiting area; seats should be arranged so that the receptionists can keep a watchful eye over the whole area. It may be wise not to arrange the seating so that inebriated patients are encouraged to lie across the chairs as a bed (waking them and attempting to remove them from the premises could result in danger to members of staff).
- All consulting rooms should be designed with a means of escape; the practitioner should be able to remove him or herself from the room without having their exit barred by a violent patient. Furniture and fittings are best fixed in order to avoid them being used as weapons.

When on home visits, all practitioners are advised to ensure that someone else is aware of their location and to be prepared to summon police assistance if their return is delayed. If the visit would seem to be 'risky' then the practitioner should not go unaccompanied.

Arguing with a patient who demands a domiciliary visit is a common pre-emptor of violence from another 'protective' family member. It is better to visit willingly than grudgingly if polite advice is not accepted by the caller.

The following suggestions may limit the need for alarm calls:

- Keep calm.
- Be respectful, tolerant and polite.
- Avoid behaviour which may provoke the patient.
- Approach slowly if essential, otherwise stay out of reach.
- Listen and try to understand – silence is sometimes of assistance.
- Ensure you have an unobstructed escape route.
- Summon aid.
- Report fully and record the incident.
- If violence is aimed at requesting drugs – remember, it is preferable for the patient to harm himself rather than yourself.

Never:

- Show hostility
- Use provocative language
- Turn your back to the patient
- Threaten to summon the police

If a receptionist suspects that a patient may cause a problem, the practitioner involved should be alerted in advance. That practitioner should then consider the circumstances and if necessary involve another practitioner in the consultation – one in front of the patient, the other perhaps 'observing' the consultation from another part of the room. If the patient objects to this, he/she can always be re-booked.

Out of hours, the door should only be answered once the identity of the caller has been confirmed and then the door should initially be left on a security chain. If a patient is threatening abuse or violence outside the practice premises, then the door should be kept locked (advisedly 'chubb' locked) and the police summoned.

Domiciliary work

Domiciliary consultations are a risk to all practitioners. Every attempt should be made to acquaint yourself with the patient's medical history before visiting and telephone numbers obtained. A colleague or the police should be alerted if the visit sounds as if there is some element of risk.

When entering a patient's house, it is wise to follow the patient into the house rather than allow them to come between you and the exit. Ensure that all passages are lit, if not, use a good torch or leave your car headlights lit.

Minimal drugs should be carried into the patient's home – if necessary, carry only essential instruments and a means of defence. This could allow the excuse of having to return to your vehicle for appropriate medication.

All staff and practitioners should be alerted if a patient is thought to present a risk.

Security and prevention of damage by terrorism

Terrorists do not always target specific businesses when they plant bombs and may plant them at random. Bombs are easily disguised

Preparing for a domiciliary visit

On accepting the visit:

- Ask whether the person is known to be violent/drunk/on drugs.
- Do you need to request an accompanying person such as a police officer or colleague?
- Do you know the area: access, lighting?
- Ensure that you have a means of contact – portable phone – and that a colleague will contact police if you are delayed.
- Equip yourself with appropriate medications, torch, map and personal alarm. It may be better to use a rucksack or carry the appropriate equipment in your pockets than to carry a briefcase – there is nothing wrong in carrying a plastic carrier bag with your necessary bits and pieces (it may not look professional, but is less tempting to a mugger!).

On arrival ensure that you park as close as possible to the patient's home and that you park in a well-lit place. Do not show your identity in your car as that might encourage theft. Avoid subways and badly-lit areas. Avoid lifts if possible.

Whenever possible, stay between the patient and the exit door – keep door unlatched if possible.

Speak calmly, efficiently and kindly. Sympathise with the patient's situation and offer help rather than anger and accusation. Don't pre-judge the patient as that will affect your manner. If drugs from your case are demanded, then it is more sensible to submit than to try and prevent theft – let the police deal with that later.

If you are attacked physically or mentally, then report the incident to the police and FHSA/Medical Board. Take note of the appropriate mechanism for dealing with violent patients issued by your FHSA or Board.

– perhaps hidden in bags, cases and other everyday containers and in out-of-the-way places. It is therefore essential that all practitioners and staff should treat any object which is unattended, unusual or out of place with suspicion.

There are four main types of bomb of which all staff should be aware:

High explosive bombs

These can kill or injure people by their blast or by causing flying debris, particularly glass. Bombs small enough to be hidden in a bag or holdall may be big enough to cause serious damage.

Vehicle bomb

A vehicle containing a high explosive bomb could be parked nearby – or a smaller bomb may be attached to the underside of a vehicle or hidden in a pannier bag attached to a bicycle.

Incendiary bomb

These are normally small and very difficult to detect and may be hidden inside a cigarette packet or cassette box. Terrorists normally target retail premises with this type of device, placing them amongst goods on display, in the pockets of clothes or inside furniture. In our practice, an incendiary device could easily be hidden as a videocassette or false set of medical records.

Postal bombs

Letter and parcel bombs are envelopes and packages designed to kill or injure people when they are opened. They may not arrive through the post. They may be delivered by hand. Any of the following signs would warn that a letter or package might contain a bomb:

- There may be grease marks on the envelope or wrapping.
- The envelope or package might smell like marzipan or machine oil.
- You may be able to see wires or foil especially if the envelope or package is damaged.
- The envelope or package may feel very heavy for its size.
- It may be heavier in some places than others.
- The envelope may be soft but the contents will feel hard.
- The package may have been delivered by hand by somebody you do not know.
- The package may be wrapped more than normal.
- There may be poor handwriting, spelling or typing.
- The envelope/package may be incorrectly addressed.
- It may come from somewhere unexpected.
- There may be too many stamps for the weight of the package.

If any person is suspicious about a package and there is an address on it, try to contact the sender. Also, enquire whether any other member of staff is expecting a package.

If anyone has any reason to suspect that a letter or package may contain a bomb it is vitally important that the following procedures are undertaken:

- Put it down gently and walk away from it.
- Request that everyone leave the area.
- Dial 999 for the police.
- Raise the alarm and request that everyone leave the surgery.
- Warn properties close by of the danger.
- Gather everyone together at a predefined meeting point.

Do not put the package/letter into anything (including water) and *do not* place anything on top of it.

Dealing with a suspicious vehicle (including bicycle) or package

If anyone becomes suspicious of any of the above, the following instructions are advised:

- Do not touch or try to remove it.
- Clear people away from the area close by.
- Dial 999 for the police.
- Raise the alarm and request that everyone leave the surgery.
- Warn properties close by of the danger.
- Gather everyone together at a meeting point.

Meeting point (A) (100 metres away)

_____

Meeting point (B) (400 metres away)

at _____

(if suspicious object is a vehicle, bicycle or bigger than a suitcase)

It is vitally important that the most senior practitioner present ensures that the practice premises are secured to prevent unauthorised entry once evacuation has taken place.

Precautions to take for basic security

- Ensure that patients do not leave personal belongings behind without your permission.
- Keep the inside and outside of the premises tidy. Do not allow rubbish to pile up as this can easily hide a bomb.
- Pay particular attention to the patient waiting areas (including the toilets) and ensure that they are kept tidy.
- Bushes should not become overgrown as these are also good cover for a bomb.

Be on your guard

Look out for suspicious or unusual behaviour and report anything which seems wrong or out of place. Question people who are in an area where they should not be and in particular look out for the following suspicious behaviour:

- Someone leaving a package or other object in an unlikely place (e.g. a doorway or flowerbed).
- Someone *placing* rather than *dropping* something into a litter bin.

Dealing with telephone warnings

If you receive a telephone warning that a bomb has been planted on the premises or somewhere else try to obtain as much information as possible from this call. Please use the checklist (see Appendix L) provided as the information gained may help the police to trace the caller and find the bomb.

If the caller tells you that the bomb is on the premises you will need to decide whether the threat is serious. There are no hard and fast rules but you should take into account whether the practice is at risk from a particular terrorist group. You should also think about the call itself. If, for example, the caller is drunk or a child then you may decide that the call is not serious.

On 5 November 1994 BT launched their Call Return service. You simply dial 1471 and a message system in the telephone network will tell you the telephone number of the last caller. Call Return will register most BT telephone numbers – even if they are ex-directory.

In *all* cases, whether or not you think the threat is serious, you should:

- Phone the police immediately.
- Decide whether to search or evacuate the area under threat.

Searching and evacuating the property

If you receive a bomb threat you will have to decide whether or not to evacuate the property immediately or to search the property first and then move everybody out if you find something suspicious. The police will not normally search the building as they would not know the layout and places where a bomb could be hidden. In addition, they would not know what should or should not be in a particular place. However, they would give advice on searching, evacuating and re-entering the building.

When searching you must be very thorough. Check the whole of the floor area, furniture and fittings right up to the ceiling, cloakrooms, toilets and passageways. Do not forget to include the car park and other areas around the building.

You are looking for something that should not be there, something that is out of place, something that nobody can recognise or explain.

If you find something that you think may be a bomb, move everybody away from it. Call the police if you have not already done so. *Do not touch or move the suspicious object.*

Re-entering the property

If you have evacuated the property without searching it and there has not been an explosion, a decision will need to be made about re-entering. This decision will be made by the most senior practitioner present.

No-one should be allowed to re-enter the building before it has been thoroughly searched.

If a time was given for the explosion over the telephone, at least one hour after that time must be allowed before a search commences.

Immunisation and protection

Although most patients attending the practice suffer only common infective diseases or physical injuries, there are risks attached which practice staff should protect against. Infective diseases include:

- Rubella (german measles)
- Chicken pox
- Measles
- Mumps
- Glandular fever
- Tonsillitis
- Bronchitis
- Diarrhoeas
- Influenza

Occasionally patients may attend with rarer or more infective diseases including:

- TB
- Hepatitis
- HIV
- Typhoid
- Meningitis

The practice policy should recommend that:

1 **All female** practice staff should ensure that they have immunity to Rubella if of child-bearing age. This can be checked by a blood test either through the practice or through the employee's own practitioner.
2 **Close contact** with patients should be avoided.
3 **Children and adults** who specify that they may have one of the above diseases should be segregated to a separate waiting area and the practitioner advised of their arrival and situation.
4 **All staff** should be offered the opportunity of immunisation against influenza annually at no cost to themselves.
5 **All housekeeping** staff and clinical staff should be offered immunisation against hepatitis B and hepatitis A.
6 **Contact with any bodily fluid** should not be made. Latex protection gloves must be worn.
7 **Reception and housekeeping staff** should not handle any pathology specimen or medical instrument unless it is known to be clean.

Notes

See Appendix B for suggested individual employee personal risk assessment and Appendix D for employee health record form.

11

Waste disposal procedure

The disposal of waste of all types needs to be considered by those working in primary care. It is not just a matter of depositing waste in a domestic dustbin and expecting the bin-man to take it away as this would expose the refuse collector to considerable risk of harm – both from physical injury and infection – and also risk the release of confidential information about patients. For GPs working in contract with the FHSA or Medical Board, all costs of refuse collection are reimbursed and there would seem to be no reasonable excuse to avoid effective disposal of waste.

The premises will need to be registered under Duty of Care Regulations for the safe disposal of any waste it generates. The appointed collector/receiver of waste will need to be identified under each specific waste category below. The Duty of Care Regulations are part of the Environmental Protection Act which ensures that wastes are stored, treated, transported and disposed of in any way to maximise the protection of the environment. Any waste produced from any business, industrial or commercial premises, is defined as controlled waste.

The policies recommended for the disposal of various types of waste are outlined below.

Contaminated sharps

On-site storage

- In plastic containers coloured yellow and white with secure fittings and able to be safely sealed without coming into contact with contents. Containers to comply with BS7320.
- These containers to be known as 'sharps bins' and must always be kept above child height.
- Containers should not be overfilled to the extent that they cannot be automatically self sealed.
- No attempt should ever be made to insert fingers into the sharps bin.

Authorised collector

The authorised collector of contaminated sharps is:

    Name:
    Address:
    Telephone:
    Fax:
    Contact:
    Licence or registration number:
    Term of contract:

Clinical waste

On-site storage

- All clinical waste, including any material which has come into contact with bodily fluid other than sharps defined above, is deposited in yellow clinical waste sacks. The sacks are tied firmly at the neck and a descriptive label attached.

Authorised collector

The authorised collector of clinical waste is:

    Name:
    Address:
    Telephone:
    Fax:
    Contact:
    Licence or registration number:
    Term of contract:

Paper waste

On-site storage
Paper waste is stored in black plastic sacks, tied either by itself or

with string. These sacks are then placed in a metal container with a close-fitting, self-closing, rubber lid[1].

Authorised collector

The authorised collector of the waste is:

    Name:
    Address:
    Telephone:
    Fax:
    Contact:
    Licence or registration number:
    Term of contract:

Confidential information

On-site storage

Any confidential information regarding a patient or any other confidential information is shredded first before being placed with other paper waste.

Paper waste is stored in black plastic sacks, tied either by itself or with string. These sacks are then placed in a metal container with a close-fitting, self-closing, rubber lid.

Authorised collector

The authorised collector of the waste is:

    Name:
    Address:
    Telephone:
    Fax:
    Contact:
    Licence or registration number:
    Term of contract:

Control of Substances Hazardous to Health (COSHH)

The Control of Substances Hazardous to Health (COSHH) covers all substances which have a potential for causing harm to people's health. It is a requirement of the regulations that employers make COSHH assessments of all such substances coming into the business, being used in the business or being manufactured by the business. The assessments are designed to ensure that harm does not come to anyone as a result of coming into contact with such substances.

Scope

Within the primary care setting the COSHH assessments will be carried out by the safety liaison officer who will take advice as appropriate from other professionals.

The COSHH assessment procedure covers all chemicals and substances hazardous to health used on the premises and by practitioners on their domiciliary visits. Each identified chemical has a fact sheet which is filed with the health and safety documentation and also sited in the cleaning store cupboard. The fact sheet includes information about the composition of the product as well as handling, disposal and first aid precautions.

Document control

Blank COSHH fact sheets need to be kept, for ready access, either within the storage area or perhaps in the COSHH section of the health and safety file. As product information arrives, the fact sheets are removed, updated and replaced. Out of date fact sheets are destroyed. COSHH fact sheets should be checked every three to six months.

Responsibilities

It is the responsibility of all staff to be aware of possible dangers to their health when handling any substance. Awareness of the safety precautions is paramount.

It is the responsibility of all staff to wear any protective clothing or equipment supplied for use when handling substances.

It is the responsibility of the safety liaison officer to ensure that COSHH assessment notices are displayed in the appropriate place in order that all staff are aware of the risks.

It is the responsibility of the safety liaison officer to ensure accurate and up to date information is given for all substances.

Audit

This procedure needs to be subject to a regular documented audit carried out by the quality manager or safety liaison officer twice a year. Each audit will include:

- Knowledge of the procedure
- Adequacy of records
- Actions taken

This audit will be reported back to all practitioners and staff within 30 days of being undertaken and a plan made for corrective action if it is found that staff are unaware of the procedure or that materials are being used without being subject to a COSHH assessment.

Example COSHH fact sheets

It is often difficult to know what needs to be included on a fact sheet for substances used in primary care. Some examples of factsheets for types of chemicals or substances used in primary care are included in the following pages.

COSHH fact sheets	Substance name: Lyptosol pine disinfectant
Issue no:	Date issued:
Authorised by:	Page 1 of 8

Description of substance:
Clear liquid.

What is the substance used for?
General purpose disinfectant – non-food-preparation areas. Mainly for cleaning floors and surfaces.

What are the dangers of the substance?
Burns skin and eyes.

What is the suggested corrective action?
Wash off skin. Irrigate eyes for at least 10 minutes and seek medical advice.

Where is the substance used?
Throughout the surgery.

Who by?
Housekeeping staff.

Where is the substance stored?
Cleaning store in the boiler room.

How much is stored at any one time?
Two bottles of 5 litres.

Is the storage area kept locked?
Yes.

Who has access to the key?
Any member of staff.

Conditions of use:
To be used only by members of housekeeping staff following the dilution instructions on the bottle. It is not to be mixed with any other cleaning agent. It should *not* be used at surgery peak times or in close proximity to other people.

How often is the substance used?
Daily.

What control methods are in place?
Rubber gloves are to be worn.

Assessment of exposure:
Minimal exposure advised.

COSHH fact sheets (HS-22b)	Substance name: Lifeguard disinfectant
Issue no:	Date issued:
Authorised by:	Page 2 of 8

Description of substance:
Amber liquid containing quaternary ammonium.

What is the substance used for?
General purpose disinfectant for use in sinks, WCs, etc.

What are the dangers of the substance?
Burns skin and eyes.

What is the suggested corrective action?
Rinse immediately with water and seek medical advice.

Where is the substance used?
Throughout the surgery premises.

Who by?
Housekeeping staff.

Where is the substance stored?
Cleaning store in the boiler room.

How much is stored at any one time?
Two bottles of 5 litres.

Is the storage area kept locked?
Yes.

Who has access to the key?
Any member of staff.

Conditions of use.
To be used only by members of housekeeping staff following the dilution instructions on the bottle. It is not to be used when the practice is busy or in close proximity to other people. It is *not* to be mixed with any other chemical or cleaning agent.

How often is the substance used?
Daily.

What control methods are in place?
Rubber gloves are to be worn.

Assessment of exposure:
Minimal contact necessary.

COSHH fact sheets (HS-22c)	Substance name: Lyptosol bleach
Issue no:	Date issued:
Authorised by:	Page 3 of 8

Description of substance:
Clear liquid –5% available chlorine.

What is the substance used for?
Cleaning.

What are the dangers of the substance?
Irritation to the eyes and skin. Contact with acid liberates toxic gas.

What is the suggested corrective action?
Wash off splashes with cold water.

Where is the substance used?
Floors and surfaces; WC bowls.

Who by?
Housekeeping staff.

Where is the substance stored?
Cleaning store in the boiler room.

How much is stored at any one time?
Two bottles of 5 litres.

Is the storage area kept locked?
Yes.

Who has access to the key?
All staff members.

Conditions of use:
To be used only by members of housekeeping staff in accordance with manufacturer's instructions. *It must not be mixed with any other cleaning agent.* It should only be used when there are few members of the public on the premises. It should be used away from other people. Adequate ventilation must be present to ensure there is no build-up of possible chlorine gas.

How often is the substance used?
Daily.

What control methods are in place?
Rubber gloves must be worn. Contact with acidic liquids should be avoided.

Assessment of exposure:
Minimal risk due to minimal exposure.

COSHH fact sheets (HS-22d)	Substance name: Taski Combistak
Issue no:	Date issued:
Authorised by:	Page 4 of 8

Description of substance:
Clear liquid – neutral detergent for automatics.

What is the substance used for?
Washing the floors.

What are the dangers of the substance?
Burns skin and eyes. Harmful if swallowed.

What is the suggested corrective action?
Wash off skin. Flush out eyes and seek medical advice. If swallowed, drink one or two cups of water or milk and seek medical advice.

Where is the substance used?
On solid floor surfaces.

Who by?
Housekeeping staff.

Where is the substance stored?
In the cleaning cupboard.

How much is stored at any one time?
One bottle of 5 litres.

Is the storage area kept locked?
Yes.

Who has access to the key?
All staff members.

Conditions of use:
To be used only by members of housekeeping staff. Manufacturer's instructions should be followed. Not to be used at peak times or in close proximity to other persons.

How often is the substance used?
Daily.

What control methods are in place?
Rubber gloves must be worn.

Assessment of exposure:
Minimal risk due to minimal exposure.

COSHH fact sheets (HS-22e)	Substance name: Sun dishwasher powder
Issue no:	Date issued:
Authorised by:	Page 5 of 8

Description of substance:
A white powder containing sodium metasilicate.

What is the substance used for?
Washing dishes in the dishwasher.

What are the dangers of the substance?
Causes burns to skin and eyes. Harmful if swallowed.

What is the suggested corrective action?
Wash off and flush eyes – seek medical advice. If swallowed, milk/water should be drunk and medical advice sought.

Where is the substance used?
In the kitchenette.

Who by?
Reception, administration and housekeeping staff.

Where is the substance stored?
Under the sink in the kitchenette in a child-proof container.

How much is stored at any one time?
One container of 3 kg.

Is the storage area kept locked?
No.

Who has access to the key?
Not applicable.

Conditions of use:
Care should be taken to avoid powder coming into contact with skin. Hands should be rinsed in running cold water after use.

How often is the substance used?
Twice a day on average.

What control methods are in place?
Staff are aware of risk and care is taken in pouring powder.

Assessment of exposure:
Risk of harm minimal – little exposure.

COSHH fact sheets (HS-22f)	Substance name: Mercury
Issue no:	Date issued:
Authorised by:	Page 6 of 8

Description of substance:
A silvery liquid of high density – tends to form ball-like globules.

What is the substance used for?
Not in general use – contained within sphygmomanometers (blood pressure machines) and thermometers. Breakage of these instruments may cause loss of mercury.

What are the dangers of the substance?
Mercury is a metabolic poison requiring specialist care.

What is the suggested corrective action?
If exposure to mercury vapour greater than the occupational exposure limit of 0.05 mg m^3 in 8 hours or 0.15 mg m^3 in 10 minutes, then medical advice should be sought. This is unlikely in the circumstances.
   Immediate contact with skin should involve washing with hot water and detergent.

Where is the substance used?
Present in clinical equipment in consultation rooms.

Who by?
Not applicable.

Where is the substance stored?
Not applicable.

How much is stored at any one time?
Not applicable.

Is the storage area kept locked?
No.

Who has access to the key?
Not applicable.

Conditions of use:
If spillage occurs from a clinical instrument containing mercury, then efforts to combine the droplets to one should be made using a brush, card or some similar object. Hands should not be used in direct contact with mercury. The mercury can then be drawn up into a large syringe or brushed into a container. The spilt mercury should then be placed in a well-labelled lidded plastic container. The room should be forcibly ventilated and the windows opened. Calcium hydroxide and sulphur paste can be applied to the contaminated areas, left to dry, then washed with hot water and detergent.
   The broken sphygmomanometer should be returned for repair, properly labelled and sealed. The waste mercury should be sent for reclaiming to a suitable unit – the local waste authority or environmental health officer should be consulted.

How often in the substance used?
Not applicable.

What control methods are in place?
Every attempt should be made not to break clinical equipment.

Assessment of exposure.
High risk – see exposure times above.

COSHH fact sheets (HS-22g)	Substance name: Ethanol (HIBISOL)
Issue no:	Date issued:
Authorised by:	Page 8 of 8

Description of substance:
A colourless clear liquid. Hibisol may contain a light blue or pink dye.

What is the substance used for?
Hand and surface cleansing.

What are the dangers of the substance?
Eye and skin irritation.

What is the suggested corrective action?
Wash off with water.

Where is the substance used?
For cleaning display boards in entrance lobby. For hand and surface cleansing in treatment room.

Who by?
Clinical staff.

Where is the substance stored?
In locked cupboards in treatment room.

How much is stored at any one time?
200 ml of ethanol. 500 ml of Hibisol.

Is the storage area kept locked?
Yes.

Who has access to the key?
Nursing staff, master copies kept in key cabinet.

Conditions of use:
Not applicable.

How often is the substance used?
Daily.

What control methods are in place?
General caution in use. If skin is broken, then ethanol should not be used.

Assessment of exposure:
Minimal.

Substance usage – fact card for all staff

Use of substances: RULES

1. Before using any chemical for cleaning or investigative purposes, make sure that you read the COSHH fact sheets kept in the cleaning cupboard.
2. If there is a product that does not have a fact sheet, check if it is hazardous or not. If it is hazardous it will be clearly marked with an orange sign on the label.
3. If it not hazardous, use as directed on the label.
4. If it is hazardous, ask the safety liaison officer to provide a factsheet with the relevant safety information before you use the product.
5. Check that you have all the necessary protective clothing or equipment.
6. If there is no safety clothing or equipment available, ask the safety liaison officer to provide the appropriate items.
7. Follow any instructions on the fact sheet regarding dilution.
8. Check that you know the first aid steps in case of an accident.
9. Check that the chemical that you are going to use is appropriate for the job you are going to do.
10. Make sure that you return the chemicals to the appropriate place in the cupboard. Hazardous substances should always be stored and used out of the reach of members of the public, especially infants.
11. Always lock the storage cupboard after use.

Notes

1 For example, a dustbin or 'Eurobin'

12

Cleaning the premises

Interior

The primary care centre is a place where members of the public attend with the hope of becoming well or avoiding disease. High expectations are held by the public that such a place should be clean, and be seen to be cleaned. Staff working in the surgery also expect a clean place of work.

When cleaning is in progress, particularly when floors are likely to be wet, hazard signs should be posted at the entrance to the premises and at any other site of danger.

Floors

All floors should be cleaned at least twice a week in the consulting rooms and offices. Floors in the general corridors and waiting rooms will need to be cleaned daily.

Walls

Interior walls, ceilings and light fittings will require cleaning at suitable intervals – at least quarterly.

Work surfaces

Will be cleaned before and after use in the treatment room by the clinical staff.

Refrigerators

Will be cleaned in rotation on a six weekly cycle. The fridge in the kitchenette, which is used for food storage, will need to be cleaned fortnightly.

Sanitary fittings

Will be cleaned daily and at any other time that they are found to be dirtied.

Cleaning vomit/urine/faeces, etc.

Occasionally a patient causes a hazard as a result of illness. If this occurs, the area should be isolated using hazard signs kept with the cleaning materials. Rubber gloves should be worn and the area cleaned with suitable cleaning agents, taking note of any appropriate COSHH warnings. Members of staff or public should not be allowed to come into contact with the area until the site has been inspected to ensure that there is no remaining health hazard.

Exterior

Steps and passageways

Brushing daily should be adequate.

Windows

Windows should be cleaned inside and out periodically as the need arises and on regular basis planned with the practice management to ensure access to the premises.

Plates and signs

Will be cleaned weekly.

Environmental hazards

Ice/snow/leaves, etc.

When weather conditions pose a risk to users of the premises – for example, when wet leaves are lying on the steps – then the first person to open the premises will clear the hazard before members of the public and other staff members arrive. If the hazard cannot be cleared quickly, then suitable warnings should be posted either side of the hazard.

Gritting or salting may be appropriate to prevent the formation of ice on the access paths to the premises.

Conclusion

Within primary care – a discipline which can encompass dentistry, chiropody, osteopathy, acupuncture and general medical practice – there are many dangers to practitioner, employees and the patients. For many years such dangers have been managed reactively and most practitioners have made little conscious effort to ensure that their practices have undergone a full health risk and safety risk assessment.

The contents of this text are never likely to be comprehensive, but I hope that they have been able to provide some practical indications and guidance as to how risks should be considered and appropriately managed in order to reduce the likely effect of that risk.

Primary care is an expanding field with more and more skills being undertaken 'in the field'. Active health and safety management requires a little lateral thinking and consideration of likely effects of any procedure or use of particular pieces of equipment.

There is a cost attached to sensible health and safety precautions. There is the investment in time necessary to plan and consider a health and safety policy. There is the time and cost involved in training staff about the importance and procedures involved. There is the cost of additional equipment – both in protecting and preventing – which will prove necessary as a result of implementation of a suitable policy. However, the benefits will be multiple – not only in the knowledge that your practice is a much healthier place in which to work and to which your patients can bring their problems – there should also be less ill health in staff and practitioners and there will be lower costs in litigation.

Appendix A

NHS Safety Notices

There is at least one set of the following NHS General Medical Services Safety Information Notices. These are kept referenced with the controlled copy of this health and safety guidance book.

Date	Ref	Topic
07/87	FPN 439	**Pedobaby Baby Meter**: risk of injury
02/88	FPN 446	**Mothercare Steel Safety Gate**: risk of instability
02/88	FPN 447	**Vickers Medical Models 20 & 60 Resuscitaires**: need for vigilance in use
05/89	FPN 604	**Keymed KC-10 Endoscope Disinfection Station (Issue 5)**: modification to handpump top seal retaining clip to prevent expulsion of glutaraldehyde
07/89	FPN 481	**Medical Gas Cylinders**: safety and care in their storage, handling and use
08/89	FPN 485	**Daniels Health Care 5 litre sharps bins**: joint failures
08/89	FPN 486	**Patient Couches**: risk of raisable head section collapse
08/89	FPN 487	**Wheelchair Safety Awareness**
03/92	FPN 561	**Glutaraldehyde Disinfectants**: use and management
06/92	FPN 566	**Diathermy Footswitches**: incidents of failure
06/92	FPN 568	**Transportable Steam Sterilizers**: maintenance, inspection and insurance
11/92	FPN 575	**Used Sharps Containers – Labco, 1 Gallon Cinbin**: potential infection risk
10/92	FPN 576	**Sanderson Autoclave**: cracks in bell locking mechanism screws
10/92	FPN 577	**SLT/Sigmacon System**: incidents with contact laser surgery delivery systems

10/92	FPN 578	**Terumo 10 ml Hypodermic Syringes Code BS-10ES**: manufacturer's recall of certain batches
02/93	FPN 579	**Robinson Healthcare 'Cameo' Press-on Maternity Pads Code 43910 – Sterile**: manufacturer's recall of all batches produced prior to October 1992
02/93	FPN 580	**MSE Mistral 2000 Centrifuge**: serial nos SG91/03/161 to SG91/10/291 – lid may fall spontaneously during loading/unloading with risk of injury to operator
02/93	FPN 582	**Cap Ltd Rookwood (DH) Seating**: requirements for reinforcement in certain applications
02/93	FPN 583	**Farley's Sterilised Water RTF**: batches 236EA, 239AB, 241AA, 241AB
03/93	FPN 584	**Bacteriological Culture Swabs**: need for adequate assurance of sterility
03/93	FPN 585	**Fresenius A2008 C and Dialysis Machines**: inactive high venous pressure alarms
03/93	FPN 586	**Carbon Dioxide Cylinders**: inappropriate user
03/93	FPN 587	**Haemodialysis Equipment**: cancellation of alarms by the user
03/93	FPN 589	**Anaesthetic Machines**: service induced fault
05/93	FPN 590	**Portex Thermovent BVF (Bacterial/Viral Filter) and intubation minipack**: manufacturer's recall
05/93	FPN 591	**Central Venous Catheters**: degradation of silicone tubing by alcohol-based antiseptics
05/93	FPN 592	**Life Sciences International (Europe) Ltd IEC 'Spinette' Centrifuge**: risk of electric shock – remove from use
05/93	FPN 593	**Blease Medical Ltd Front Line Anaesthetic Machines**: occlusion of machine gas delivery system pipelines
05/93	FPN 594	**Needles for blood collection by the evacuated blood sample tube and by the syringe and needle methods**: re-sheathing after use and improper disposal: possibility of inadvertent re-use and risk of infection
05/93	FPN 595	**Chubb Fire Extinguisher**: risk of cracks to plastic coating of gas cartridge
07/93	FPN 597	**Ohmeda OAV Ventilator**: air entrainment caused patient awareness

07/93   FPN 598   **Syringe Pumps**: uncontrolled infusion
07/93   FPN 599   **Prestige Medical Series 2000 (Selected Models) Clinical Autoclaves and Kavo Supra Klave Model L2072**: risk of lid detaching whilst under pressure
07/93   FPN 600   **Anglia Vale Medical Ltd Mouthcare Tray – Code 2668**: manufacturer's recall
07/93   FPN 601   **Rocialle Medical Ltd Oral Hygiene Packs**: manufacturer's recall
08/93   FPN 602   **Flexicare Medical Ltd/S&W Vickers Ltd**: S&W Vickers 24% Venturi Products: Ventimask 24%; Venticare 24%; Venturi Barrel 24% – product recall of all batches
08/93   FPN 603   **Endoscope Washer Disinfectors**: re-contamination of equipment
08/93   FPN 605   **HG Wallace Ltd, IV Cannulae – Code 519 16G Labelling error batch 211292**: recall
08/93   FPN 606   **Kendal Curity 8.5mm Tracheal Tube**: tube splitting at the proximal end
09/93   FPN 607   **Fry Surgical International Ltd Bladders for Stille Tourniquet**: batch dates 1993–03 to 1993–06. Air/gas supply hose may detach from bladder spigot during use.
09/93   FPN 608   **Degradation of Plastics IV Catheters** due to interactions with solvent based spray dressings and disinfectants
09/93   FPN 609   **MSE Mistral 3000 Series Bench Top Centrifuges**: software upgrade to improve safety
09/93   FPN 610   **Pregstik Pregnancy Test Kits – Organon Laboratories Ltd**: recall because of ambiguous results
09/93   FPN 611   **Mercury Contamination of Baby Incubators**: the need for vigilance
09/93   FPN 612   **Kendall Curity 8.5mm Tracheal Tubes**: quarantined in accordance with hazard notice (93)23
09/93   FPN 613   **Viomedex Ltd VX 700 Enteral Nutrition Pumps**: modification to internal circuit board mounting
09/93   FPN 614   **Care of the Intavent Ltd Laryngeal Mask**: new guidelines for their care
09/93   FPN 615   **Scott Western FL40 Instrument Washer**: potential risk of scorching to wiring

10/93	FPN 616	**Stihler Electronic Gmbh/Althin Medical Ltd Electrically Heated Mattress**: system type Astopad OPT 100 – possible severe overheating without warning
10/93	FPN 618	**Vernon-Carus Ltd Sterile Detectable Swabs and Image Intensifier Hoods**: manufacturer's recall of affected batches
10/93	FPN 619	**Steriseal, Sorbsan Sterile Calcium Alginate Packing Code 1411, Batch 190793**: manufacturer's recall
09/93	FPN 621	**Graseby Medical Ltd PCA Extension Set 0128-0085-1**: Recall of lots B/193; B/245; B/270; B/320 – discontinue use
09/93	FPN 622	**Ohmeda Modulus CD Anaesthetic Machine**: serial numbers listed in appendix to FPN 622. Non-invasive blood pressure (NIBP) monitor failure
11/93	FPN 624	**Daniels Health Care Community Sharps Containers**: assembly of incompatible lids and bases
11/93	FPN 625	**Laerdal Silicone Resuscitators**: inadvertent positive expiratory end pressure (PEEP)
12/93	FPN 626	**Sharps Containers**: use and management
12/93	FPN 627	**Little Sister 2 Autoclave:** Failure of solid state relay, leading to overheating
12/93	FPN 629	**Vial Medical SE Syringe Pumps manufactured before 1986**: may cease to infuse although continuing to indicate normal infusion
12/93	FPN 630	**Nikomed 4050 Pre-gelled ECG Electrodes**: difficulty in removal of backing cover
12/93	FPN 631	**Liquid Nitrogen Cooling and Storage of Biological Materials**: risk reduction
12/93	FPN 632	**Nunc 'Crotube' Vials Stored in Liquid Nitrogen**: risk reduction
12/93	FPN 633	**Foster Refrigerators**: risk of microprocessor catching fire
12/93	FPN 634	**Graseby Medical Limited MS16A, MS26, MS27 & MS30 Ambulatory Syringe Pumps**: possible over infusion if the sounder becomes loose and contacts the rate control switches
01/94	FPN 637	**Use of Hospital Bed Safety Sides and Side Rails**
02/94	FPN 640	**Vi-tal Syringe Pumps**: withdrawal of technical support and spares

02/94	FPN 641	**Lifepack 10 Defibrillator/Monitor Manufactured by Physio Control**: manufacturer's modification
02/94	FPN 642	**S&W Vickers Resuscitaire 165 Flowmeter Control Valve**: over-tightening of valve knob may cause damage
02/94	FPN 643	**S&W Vickers Resuscitaires**: defective pin index yokes used for the location of gas cylinders
04/94	FPN 647	**Becton Dickinson Prog. 1 and 2 Syringe Pumps**: manufactured before 1990. Upgrade facility to high risk category recommendations
05/94	FPN 649	**Wheelchairs**: Safety of Obsolete Equipment: failure of a trigger switch on an old model of an attendant controlled electric wheelchair
04/94	FPN 650	**S&W Vickers DMS 600 and DMS 700 Series Defibrillators**: modification to the carrying handle
05/94	FPN 651	**GE Lighting 'Pluslife' 240 Incandescent Lamps**: explosion risk
06/94	FPN 654	**Instruments and Appliances used in the Vagina and Cervix**: recommended methods for decontamination
06/94	FPN 655	**Dry Heat Sterilizers: Purchase, Maintenance and Use:** incorrect maintenance and use of dry heat sterilizers may result in performance requirements not being achieved.
06/94	FPN 656	**'Sapona' Office Equipment Foam Cleaner**: risk of can rupture
06/94	FPN 657	**Graseby Medical Limited – MS16A and MS26 Ambulatory Syringe Driver**: confusion between these two models of syringe driver has led to inappropriate infusion rates being set, leading to serious over-infusion with potential fatal consequences
7/94	FPN 658	**Infusion Pumps: Incidents caused by fluid spillage and drop damage:** checks should be made by an appropriately qualified person prior to being used if the infusion pump has been subject to a fluid spill
7/94	FPN 659	**Welmed P1000, P2000, P3000 and P4000 Syringe Pumps**: mandatory upgrade of identified pumps due to the possibility of no infusion and delayed alarm at low flow rates

7/94	FPN 660	**3M Defibrillator Pads Type 2345, 2346, 2345N and 2346N**: manufacturer's recall
7/94	FPN 661	**13 Amp Rewirable and non-Rewirable (Moulded) Plugs**: non-compliance with safety regulations
8/94	FPN 662	**Cow and Gate 470 Enteral Feeding Pump**: change of delivery rate following momentary interruption of the mains supply
8/94	FPN 663	**Jackson Instantaneous Hot Water Boiler**: potential risk of scalding
9/94	FPN 664	**Gambro Haemodialysis AK10 Systems**: prevention of inadvertent fluid ingress
9/94	FPN 666	**Kamplex Models AT22 and AT24 Impedance Audiometers**: risk of inadvertent re-calibration
9/94	FPN 667	**Diathermy Injury During Laparoscopic Surgery**: potential causes of unintended diathermy injury
9/94	FPN 669	**Polyurethane-Coated Breast Implants**: potential release of a probable carcinogenic degradation product following breakdown of the polyurethane foam *in vivo*
10/94	FPN 671	**Analogue Addressable Fire Alarm Panel**: system failure due to jamming of the printer
10/94	FPN 674	**Hewlett-Packard Portable Monitor Type 1275A**: carrying handle can become detached
10/94	FPN 675	**Photon Beard Halogen Luminaire**: potential risk of short circuit
10/94	FPN 676	**Low Income Optical Voucher Scheme**: extension of automatic entitlement to help with health costs to recipients of Disability Working Allowance (DWA) whose capital is £8000 or less
11/94	FPN 677	**Haag Streit 900 Slit Lamp**: risk of electric shock from the power connector
11/94	FPN 678	**Portable, Cordless & Cellular Telephones**: interference with medical devices
11/94	FPN 679	**Syringe Pumps**: Uncontrolled infusion due to siphonage: reports of uncontrolled infusion due to siphonage (free) flow, in some cases resulting in death. To prevent this, users must ensure that the syringe plunger and barrel are securely attached to the syringe driver before and during infusion

12/94	FPN 681	**Vernon Thompson Suction Apparatus:** **Upgrade:** offered to meet current standards of electrical safety by protecting against the ingress of fluids
10/94	FPN 682	**Wheathampstead Sales Services Limited:** **Handley Clockwork Syringe Driver:** potential for overinfusion during single fault condition: risk of patient injury or death
11/94	FPN 683	**Baxter Healthcare Ltd: CA Haemodialysers:** **Codes RTM 1731, RTM 1732, RTM 1733, RTM 1735, RTM 1736 – Various lots:** adverse patient reaction. Staff to check stocks for any of above numbers. Withdraw from use any affected stock for collection and replacement or credit
1/95	FPN 684	**Teletronics Pacing Systems Accufix Atrial 'J' Pacing Leads. Models 330-801, 329-701 and 033-812:** fracture of pacing lead retention wire, possibly leading to perforation and atrial and aortic wall and causing cardiac tamponade and/or haemothorax
1/95	FPN 686	**High Tech Health Care for Patients at Home:** re: provision via form FP10 of high-tech home healthcare packages
12/94	FPN 687	**Glade Plug-ins electrical Air Fresheners:** recall notice

Appendix B

Personal health and safety records

Individual health and safety assessments of staff members.

Name:
Post:
Date of assessment:
Risks:

Recommendations:

A checklist for health and safety

1. Is there a written health and safety policy?
2. Is there a nominated safety officer?
3. Is there a specified fire evacuation procedure?
4. Is there a first aid kit?
5. Is there a trained first aider?
6. Is there an accident book?
7. Is the certificate of employer's liability current and displayed?
8. Is the Health and Safety Act poster displayed at the surgery giving the address and telephone number of the local Health and Safety Executive?
9. Has individual risk assessment been undertaken for each member of staff?
10. Have steps been taken to minimise risk for VDU operators?
11. Is there adequate ventilation of toilets and all surgery rooms?
12. Is the lighting effective?
13. Is there an emergency lighting system?
14. Is there a means of alerting others of fire?
15. Are smoke detectors installed?
16. Is there a secure place to store staff possessions?
17. Is there a means for members of staff to obtain water for drinking purposes?
18. Have all portable electrical appliances been checked by an appropriately registered electrician?
19. Is there an effective security system in the surgery with a means of calling for assistance?
20. Is there a system for ensuring sterilisation of clinical equipment?
21. Have appropriate staff been offered and immunised against hepatitis?
22. Is there a system for disposal of sharps in a safe manner?
23. Have duty of care regulations been invoked for clinical waste and clinical sharps?
24. Are pathological specimens handled in a safe manner and appropriately labelled?

25. Is protective equipment provided for staff to wear?
26. Has an assessment been made of chemicals, substances and microbiological hazards likely to become hazardous to health?
27. Is there a system of audit of health and safety policies?

Appendix D

Employee and Practitioner Health Record Form

Name:	Date of birth:	Date completed:	Staff reference number:
Tuberculosis testing	BCG Mantoux	Date Date	Result Result
Hepatitis B	Initial testing Immunisations	Past exposure? 1: 2: 3: Booster1: Booster2: Booster3:	Carrier? Antibody levels: Date:
Tetanus	Primary course? Y/N	Booster (every 10 years recommended)	Booster date:
Polio	Primary course? Y/N	Booster (every 10 years recommended)	Booster date:
Diphtheria	Primary course? Y/N	Booster? (low dose diphtheria toxoid advised)	Booster date:
Typhoid	Primary course? Y/N	Dose 1 Dose 2 Dose 3	Booster date:
Rubella	Primary course?	Antibodies checked	Booster date: (ensure no risk of pregnancy for 3 months afterwards)
Hepatitis A	Primary course? Y/N Antibody levels?	Dose 1 Dose 2 Dose 3	Booster date
Other vaccinations (particularly Rabies if animal handling)			
Influenza	Annual immunisation	Date: Date: Date: Date:	

Screening past medical history			
Have you ever had any industrial or occupational disease?	Y/N	Details	Outcome
Have you ever had an accident at work?	Y/N	Details	Outcome
Have you ever had? Chicken pox Shingles Typhoid Tuberculosis Hepatitis or yellow jaundice Malaria Herpes (cold sores)	Y/N	Details	
Do you have any disabilities or infirmities which may affect your work in any way?	Y/N	Details	
If your work involves regular use of a VDU (visual display unit), then please answer these questions? Do you wear lenses or spectacles for VDU work? When did you last have an eye test? Do you have any colour vision defects? Have you been tested for colour vision defects?	Y/N	Details	
I declare that the statements on this form are true and complete to the best of my knowledge.	Signed:	Dated:	

Review date and signature   Actions recommended

....

....

....

Appendix E

Further reading and references

Seating at Work	HSE, ISBN 0-11-885431-3, HS(G) 57
The Lifting of Patients in the Health Service	HSC, ISBN 0-11-883745-1
Medico-Legal Aspects of General Practice	MDU Ltd, ISBN 0-902094-36-X
The Safe Use of Portable Electrical Apparatus (Electrical Safety)	HSE, ISBN 0-11-885590-5, C80
Basic Life Support – Marsden	BMJ, Volume 299, pp. 442–4, 1989
Advanced Life Support – Chamberlain	BMJ, Volume 299, 1989
Control of Substances Hazardous to Health	HSC, ISBN 0-11-885698-7 L5
COSHH Assessments	HSE, ISBN 0-11-885470-4
Control of Substances Hazardous to Health	Department of Health, ISBN 0-11-321262-3
A Guide to the Health and Safety at Work Act	HSC, ISBN 0-11-885555-7 L1
Safe Disposal of Clinical Waste	HSC, ISBN 0-11-886355-X
Employers Liability (Compulsory Insurance) Act 1969	ISBN 0-10-545769-8
First Aid at Work	HSC, ISBN 0-11-885536-0, COP42

Control of Legionellosis (including Legionnaire's Disease)	HSE, ISBN 0-11-885660-X, HS(G)70
Work Equipment – Guidance on Regulations	HSE, ISBN 0-11-886332-0
Display Screen Equipment Work	HSE, ISBN 0-11-886331-2
General Medical Services Committee Guidance on Combating Violence in General Practice	General Medical Services Committee, Tavistock Square, London
Streetwise and Safe	Medical Imprint, 55 North Wharf Road, London W2 1LA
The Prevention or Control of Legionellosis (including Legionnaire's Disease)	HSC, ISBN 0-11-885659-2, L8
Office, Shops and Railway Premises Act 1963	ISBN 0-10-850111-6
Management of Health and Safety at Work	HSC, ISBN 0-11-886330-4
Workplace Health, Safety and Welfare	HSC, ISBN 0-11-886333-9
Immunisation against infectious disease	Department of Health, HMSO
Infection Control in Dentistry	BDA occasional paper, issue number 2, July 1993, 64 Wimpole Street, London W1M 8AL

The law regarding offences against the person, public order and advice on procedures to be followed after an attack by a patient or relative

Under current law, offences occurring in different places are covered by separate legislation.

Incidents outside or on practice premises

Provided the practice premises are not classed as a 'dwelling house', then section 4 of the Public Order Act 1986 (England and Wales) states that it is an offence to 'use towards another person threatening, abusive or insulting words or behaviour with intent to cause that person to believe that immediate unlawful violence will be used against him or by any person'. Section 5 of the same Act makes it an offence 'to use threatening, abusive or insulting words or behaviour within the hearing or sight of a person likely to be caused harassment, alarm or distress.'

In Scotland there is no equivalent Act to the Public Order Act although the same areas are covered by the Civic Government (Scotland) Act 1982. Scottish Police can also invoke a common law offence of 'breach of the peace' and this has the advantage of being applied to a private house as well as a public place.

Incidents in the patient's home

The public order act does not apply to a residential property. The Offences Against the Person Act 1861 (England and Wales only) covers actual assault and assault causing bodily harm. Theoretically, touching someone without their consent can constitute assault.

In Scotland, assault is dealt with by common law and the crime of assault involve the attack on the person of another. An attack is the application of force which may involve either direct physical onslaught or the use of indirect means or by the use of physically threatening gestures whereby the victim must anticipate harm to him- or herself.

Action to be taken following a threatened or actual attack

Report the incident immediately to the police. It is essential to do this and to ensure that the police respect that you are making a formal complaint against the assailant. If you intend to remove this patient from your practice list (if medical or dental), then it is essential that the police have been informed.

If you are a medical or dental practitioner, then you should request that the FHSA or Medical Board remove the patient from your list. The FHSA or Medical Board will advise you of their specific requirements but you will remain responsible for the patient for 24 hours.

Ensure that all members of staff, deputising services, and other practitioners are aware of the incident.

If you are required to attend that patient again, ensure that police are present and that they accompany you to and from your car or practice.

If the assailant has not been taken into police custody, consider an injunction against the patient. This should be done through your solicitor and will restrain the offender from approaching you at the practice, your home or any other place where you may be called.

Long term

Firm action must be taken by all practitioners to discourage violence against the caring professions. There should be no discouragement to prosecution of those who attempt violence against practitioners or their staff. Similarly any attempt to deceive the practitioner by giving a false name or address should be advised to the police. Any attempt to force the prescribing of particular drugs is a serious offence and the police and local pharmacies should be advised immediately.

Violence will not be tolerated in order that practitioner–patient relationships can continue on the basis of trust.

Appendix G

Sources of documentation and help

Managing risk in general practice:
Merrett Health Risk Management Ltd
Chandos House, North Street, Brighton BN1 2RB
Tel: 01273 747272. Fax: 01273 206450.

Forms, placards and signs for the control of health and safety at work:
Chancellor Formecon
Gateway, Crewe, CW1 1YN
Tel: 01270 500800. Fax: 01270 50050.

Appendix H

NHS Injury Benefits Scheme

The NHS Injury Benefits Scheme provides temporary or permanent benefit for all NHS employees who lose remuneration because of an injury or disease applicable to their NHS employment. This benefit is also available to practitioners who contract their services to the NHS such as medical and dental practitioners.

Under the conditions of the scheme it is essential that the injury or disease was caused or acquired during the course of work. A record of specific injury, and in the case of infection, seroconversion, are helpful in establishing a case. Any worker who suspects contamination by an infected patient (e.g. hepatitis or HIV) is advised to have a serum sample taken at the time of injury for storage and possible future testing, together with follow-up samples at appropriate intervals.

Injury benefits are payable to workers, whether symptomatic or not, and are intended to compensate for loss of earning ability. For those having to give up their employment, the scheme provides a guaranteed income of up to 85 per cent of pre-injury NHS earnings. The benefits are inflation-proofed and temporary allowances are subject to taxation but the permanent allowance payable on retirement from service is not. If employment is terminated because of the relevant injury or disease, a lump sum is payable. In the case of death, dependants' benefits are allowed.

DSS Industrial Injuries Benefits Scheme

Industrial injuries disablement benefit can be paid when an employee contracts certain defined illnesses or injuries as a result of their work and where their work exposes them to such risk. For example, an employee who contracts hepatitis A or B (Prescribed Disease B8 includes hepatitis A and B) must have worked in an environment where they have had contact with human blood or blood products or a source of viral hepatitis.

The scheme covers 'employed earners' – which means anyone who works for payment under a contract to do services. The amount payable is dependent on the degree of disability. Claims must be made on the relevant documentation from the Department of Social Security.

Health and Safety Executive Offices

South west	Inter City House Mitchell Lane Victoria Street Bristol BS1 6AN	0117 929 0681
South	Priestley House Priestley Road Basingstoke RG24 9NW	01256 473181
South east	3 East Grinstead House London Road East Grinstead West Sussex RH19 1RR	01342 326922
London, north	Maritime House 1 Linton Road Barking Essex	0181 594 5522
London, south	Long Lane London SE1 4PG	0171 407 8911
East Anglia	39 Baddow Road Chelmsford Essex CM2 0HL	01245 284661
Northern home counties	14 Cardiff Road Luton LU11 1PP	01582 34121

East Midlands	5th Floor Belgrave House 1 Greyfriars Northampton NN1 2BS	01604 21233
West Midlands	McLaren Building 2 Masshouse Circus Queensway Birmingham B4 7NP	0121 200 2299
Wales	Brunel House Fitzalan Road Cardiff CF2 1SH	01222 473777
Marches	The Marches House Midway Newcastle-under-Lyme Staffordshire ST5 1DT	01782 717181
North Midlands	Birkbeck House Trinity Square Nottingham NG1 4AU	0115 947 0712
South Yorkshire and Humberside	Sovereign House 110 Queen Street Sheffield S1 2ES	0114 273 9081
West and North Yorkshire	8 St Paul's Street Leeds LS1 2LE	0113 244 6191
Greater Manchester	Quay House Quay Street Manchester M3 3JB	0161 831 7111

Merseyside	The Triad Stanley Road Bootle L20 3PG	0151 922 7211
North west	Victoria House Ormskirk Road Preston PR1 1HH	01772 59321
North east	Arden House Regent Centre Gosforth Newcastle-upon-Tyne NE3 3JN	0191 284 8448
Scotland, east	Belford House 59 Belford Road Edinburgh EH4 3UE	0131 225 1313
Scotland, west	314 St Vincent Street Glasgow G3 8XG	0141 204 2646

National Poisons Information Services

Belfast	01232 240503
Cardiff	01222 711711
Dublin	00 353 133 79969
Edinburgh	0131 229 2477
London	0171 635 9191
	0171 955 5095

Checklist ... what to do if you receive a telephone bomb threat

If possible tell someone else immediately so that they can tell one of the partners – but **DO NOT PUT DOWN THE HANDSET OR STOP THE CONVERSATION.**

Try to keep the caller talking (apologise for a bad phone line, ask him\her to speak up and so on). Get as much information as you can.

Fill in this form as you go along. Ask the questions below if the caller does not give you the information that you need. Try and ask them in the order they appear so that you do not miss any out.

Time of call
Where is the bomb?
What time will it go off?
What does it look like?
What kind of explosive is in the bomb?
Why are you doing this?
Who are you?

When the call has finished give this form to the most senior manager or Partner/Associate in the practice. If no such person is available, contact the police. It should be dealt with immediately. The more information you can get the easier it will be to decide whether the warning was serious or not.

Fill in these details as soon as possible

Was the caller:	How they sounded	Was the caller reading a message?
Male	Drunk	Yes
Female	Rational	No
Child	Rambling	
Young	Laughing	
Old	Accent	
Don't know	Speech Impediment (If yes, give details)	
Other noises during the call	**Did the caller use a pay phone (pay tones or coins?)**	**Did you hear the operator?**
Any noise on the phone line?	Yes	Yes
Yes	No	No
No		
If yes, give details		
Where there any interruptions to the call?	**Other noises in the background**	**Number you received the call on?**
Yes	Traffic	
No	Talk	
If yes, give details	Typing	
	Machinery	
	Aircraft	
	Music	
	Children	
Your name		

Index